THE DAY OF THE BARBARIANS

BY THE SAME AUTHOR:

The Battle: A New History of the Battle of Waterloo
Charlemagne: Father of a Continent

THE DAY OF THE BARBARIANS

THE FIRST BATTLE IN THE FALL OF THE ROMAN EMPIRE

ALESSANDRO BARBERO

Translated from the Italian by John Cullen

Atlantic Books
LONDON

First published in hardback in Great Britain in 2007 by Atlantic Books,
an imprint of Grove Atlantic Ltd.

Published simultaneously in the United States of America in 2007 by
Walker Publishing Company, Inc., New York.

Originally published in Italy in 2005 by Gius, Laterza & Figli as
9 Agosto 378: Il Giorno dei Barbari.

1 3 5 7 9 8 6 4 2

A CIP catalogue record for this book is available from the British Library.

ISBN: 978 1 84354 593 4

Printed in Great Britain by MPG Books Ltd, Bodmin, Cornwall

Atlantic Books
An imprint of Grove Atlantic Ltd
Ormond House
26–27 Boswell Street
London
WC1N 3JZ

Contents

Hadrian's Wall
NORTH SEA
BRITANNIA
BALTIC
Elbe River
English Channel
Rhine River
GERMANIA
ATLANTIC OCEAN
Danube R
Tours
GALLIA
NORICUM
RAETIA
PANNO
ALPS
Rhone River
Milan
ILLYRIC
Parma
Po River
Modena
Adriatic Sea
PYRENEES
APPENINNINO
ITALIA
CORSICA
Rome
Cann
HISPANIA
Tyrrhenian Sea
SARDINIA
Reggio Calabria
SICILIA
MAURETANIA
TRIPOLITANIA
Western Roman Empire
Eastern Roman Empire
0 250 500 Miles
0 250 500 Kilometers
Lambert Conic Conformal Projection

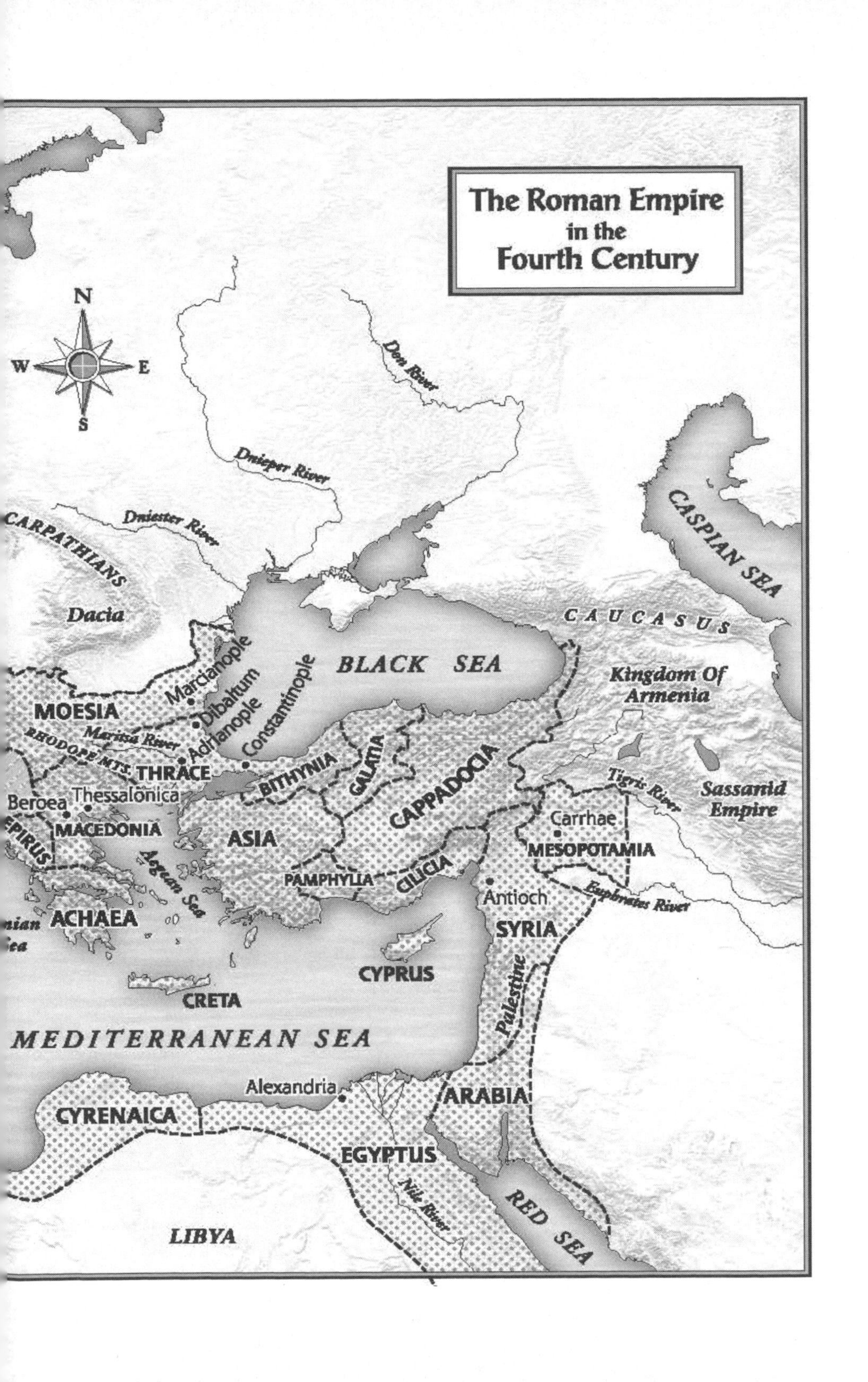
The Roman Empire in the Fourth Century
N
W
E
S
Don River
Dnieper River
Dniester River
CARPATHIANS
Dacia
CASPIAN SEA
CAUCASUS
BLACK SEA
Kingdom Of Armenia
Marcianople
Dibaltum
Adrianople
Constantinople
MOESIA
Maritsa River
RHODOPE MTS.
THRACE
BITHYNIA
GALATIA
CAPPADOCIA
Tigris River
Sassanid Empire
Beroea
Thessalonica
EPIRUS
MACEDONIA
ASIA
Carrhae
MESOPOTAMIA
Aegean Sea
PAMPHYLIA
CILICIA
Antioch
Euphrates River
ACHAEA
SYRIA
CYPRUS
Palestine
CRETA
MEDITERRANEAN SEA
Alexandria
ARABIA
CYRENAICA
EGYPTUS
Nile River
RED SEA
LIBYA

PROLOGUE

The subject of this book is a battle that changed the course of world history. It was not a famous fight like Waterloo or Stalingrad; in fact, most people have never heard of it. And yet some believe that it signified nothing less than the end of the ancient world and the beginning of the Middle Ages, because this battle set in motion the chain of events that would lead, nearly a century later, to the fall of the Western Roman Empire. That event is linked to a well-known date that forms part of our common fund of knowledge: AD 476, the year when Romulus Augustulus, the last Roman emperor of the West, was deposed. But in fact the removal of Romulus was only the final, inevitable step in a process that had begun long before. By 476, the emperor was a puppet without any effective power; the empire had already broken up and was losing one piece after another; barbarians were dominant in Gaul, in Spain, in Africa, and even in Italy; and Rome had been sacked more than once, by the Goths in 410 and again by the Vandals in 455. In short, the dissolution of the empire was already so far advanced that the deposition of the last Western emperor was not very important news. A famous essay by Arnaldo Momigliano titled "An Empire's Silent Fall" demonstrates that the so-called great event of 476, the dethronement of Romulus Augustulus, was noted by few at the time.

But if things had reached this point, if the western half of the Roman Empire had been reduced to an empty shell that a barbarian chieftain could sweep aside without eliciting a protest, it was because of a series of traumas that had begun exactly a century before. In 376, an unforeseen flood of refugees at the frontiers of the empire, and the inability of the Roman authorities to manage this emergency properly, gave rise to a dramatic conflict that was to culminate in Rome's most disastrous military defeat since Hannibal's Carthaginians destroyed the Roman army at Cannae in 216 BC.

This book recounts the battle of Adrianople, fought on August 9, 378, in what today is European Turkey and at the time was the Roman province of Thrace. In addition to telling the story of the battle, I shall try to show that it really did mark the end of one era and the beginning of another, an era in which Rome would find it harder and harder to keep the barbarians subjugated by force of arms and to keep believing itself the world's only superpower. I shall talk about the ancient world and the Middle Ages, Romans and barbarians, a multiethnic world and an empire in transformation, and about many other things besides: Christianity, for example, which by this time not only was the official religion of the Roman Empire but was making inroads among the barbarians, too, and changing them. But my central focus will be what happened there, at Adrianople in the eastern Balkans, during the course of a long summer afternoon.

I

THE ROMAN EMPIRE IN THE FOURTH CENTURY

In the year AD 378, the Roman Empire had grown to immense proportions, with geographic horizons far different from those of contemporary Europe. Today Europe is a continental civilization, open (if at all) toward the Atlantic; the Mediterranean is a boundary, and what lies beyond it is generally perceived as another civilization, another world. The Roman Empire, by contrast, coincided with the Mediterranean basin, and the sea, *mare nostrum* (our sea), was its center. The boundaries of the empire lay elsewhere: To the north, they were formed by two great rivers, the Rhine and the Danube, that to our way of thinking flow through the heart of Europe but to the Romans were border zones, the outer limits of civilization. Another great river, the Tigris, marked Rome's eastern frontier; the lands it enclosed seem distant and exotic to us, but they were part of the empire, too, and Roman functionaries, soldiers, and merchants probably felt less out of place in Mesopotamia than they did in the frigid outposts of the north. To the south, where the Romans had advanced deep into Africa and Arabia, the boundaries of the empire were the African and Arabian deserts. The Roman presence here was not confined to fortified frontier posts with garrisons of legionaries; it included city-sized commercial centers, great villas, and large estates, with olive groves and vineyards and grain fields. The Mediterranean, the central nervous system of this entire world, was crisscrossed by cargo ships carrying, for example, oil and grain from Tunisia to Rome, a metropolis of one million inhabitants who consumed an enormous quantity of food and provisions.

The lands that constituted the empire thus encompassed much more than the European provinces most familiar to our Western eyes: Spain, long since wrested from Carthage; Gaul, conquered by Julius Caesar; Britain, enveloped in the North Atlantic fog; Italy, which by the time of the battle of Adrianople had lost a portion of its status—and the privileges attendant upon that status—as the imperial center. In addition, the Roman Empire comprised the Balkan provinces, which provided Rome with its best soldiers; Asia Minor, which today we call Turkey; Syria, Palestine, and Egypt, or in other words much of the Middle East, including a portion of the Arabian Peninsula; and, finally, the North African coastal strip now known as the Maghreb. It thus comprised entire regions of the world that Europeans now consider "elsewhere"; yet those regions were at the time an integral part of the Roman world and included the richest and most civilized provinces of the empire.

Civilization's center of gravity was located in the East, and for this reason Emperor Constantine the Great had founded the city of Constantinople in AD 330 as a replacement for Rome. As we know, Constantinople became the modern city of Istanbul, the great Turkish metropolis. In our times, the admission of Turkey into Europe is a matter of controversy, but in the fourth century, Constantinople was the beating heart of the Roman Empire. In this empire, Latin, the language of the Romans, was spoken, but so was Greek; in fact, Greek was spoken more and more, because Greek was the language of the East. Latin was still, everywhere, the language of the courts and the barracks, the language in which laws were written. But in the great cities of the eastern provinces, the same cities where Christianity had known its first diffusion, the dominant language was Greek.

* * *

We are accustomed to thinking of the Roman Empire on the eve of the fourth-century barbarian invasions as an organism in an advanced stage of decay. It evokes corruption and vain display, eunuchs and concubines, refined tortures and abstract theological disquisitions: a world in both moral and material decline. In the eighteenth century, the English historian Edward Gibbon wrote a monumental study of this period, a work destined to exercise an enormous influence and to become one of the most famous historical books of all time, which he chose to call *The History of the Decline and Fall of the Roman Empire*. In reality, however, things were not quite as bad as this title implies.

The Roman Empire had two serious problems that it never managed to resolve: the continual usurpations of power by generals who had themselves acclaimed emperor by their troops, if possible after having assassinated the reigning emperor; and barbarian raids across the imperial borders. But in the fourth century, both of those problems seemed to be, comparatively speaking, under control. There had been many worse moments in the past, notably in the third century, when in the course of fifty years some twenty-three emperors succeeded to the imperial throne and almost none of them died of natural causes. During this period, the barbarian incursions reached the heart of the imperial provinces considered most secure, sowing panic in the plain of the Po River in Italy and even invading Athens; yet the empire survived.

The situation had been saved by a series of particularly energetic emperors, all of them career soldiers raised to the throne by the army, including such men as Aurelian, who built the Aurelian Wall around Rome, Diocletian, who conducted the last great persecution of the

Christians, and, naturally, Constantine the Great. These were men of action, of clear ideas and brutal methods, who used those methods to set the empire back on its feet without worrying too much about the price the population would be required to pay. They reintroduced obligatory conscription, doubled taxes, strengthened the bureaucracy and the secret police; because discontent was widespread, they instituted severe laws against desertion, tax evasion, and lèse-majesté; they transformed the emperor into a sacred, untouchable figure ordinary people didn't even have the right to look upon; they threatened dissidents with cruel and terrible punishments. In order to receive a death sentence, it wasn't necessary to go so far as to conspire against the emperor; casting his horoscope in an attempt to discover the date of his death was offense enough.

Judged by today's standards, the empire revived by these generals, the Roman Empire of the fourth century, had some distinctly disagreeable totalitarian aspects, and we are bound to think we would never have tolerated living under such tyranny. And yet the recipe worked: The empire recovered; the economy carried on; money circulated. While it's true that there were greater and more prosperous cities in the Greek East than in the Latin West, still, wherever one looks, one finds a society filled with contradictions, not an empire in decline.

* * *

In 378, Rome was not even in decline from a cultural standpoint, though it was indeed in transformation, because the fourth was the century in which the empire became Christian. In 313, Constantine had put an end to religious persecution by issuing the Edict of Milan, which, as a means of guaranteeing the prosperity of the empire, declared that all religions had to be tolerated and everyone could pray to God in his own way. Soon, however, Constantine made clear that for him the Christian religion was the one best qualified to guarantee his subjects' happiness and that the Christian church could count on solid support from the government whenever such support might be needed. After Constantine, all the Roman emperors were Christians, with a single exception: Julian, whom Christians called "the Apostate," the renegade. Traditional culture had not disappeared; the cities of the empire were still filled with rhetoricians, philosophers, and poets, many of them pagans, who kept alive the great traditions of oratory, philosophy, and classical poetry in both Latin and Greek. But pagan culture was giving ground to Christianity, which did not eradicate the ancient roots but rather gave them a new direction and new vitality.

The late fourth century encompassed the lifetimes of some of the greatest fathers of the church, the intellectuals who labored to give Christianity its philosophical foundations—and from a theoretical point of view, Christianity is a complicated religion. In 378, the year of Adrianople, St. Ambrose, though not yet forty years old, was the bishop of Milan; St. Augustine, his spiritual adventure barely begun, was a promising student in a great African city, a young man still more attached to his Manichaean sect than to the Roman Catholic Church; St. Jerome, his exciting but disappointing experience as a hermit in the Mesopotamian desert recently concluded, was in his very early thirties, preparing to return to Italy and dedicate himself to what was the truly great undertaking of his life, the translation of the Bible from Greek and Hebrew into the Latin version known as the Vulgate. In Gaul, the oldest of them all, the sexagenarian St. Martin—who slashed his cloak in half and shared it with a poor man—was trying to reconcile his vocation as a monk with the onerous office of bishop of Tours, to which he had been called by the people.

These names, along with those of the great Greek fathers, less well known to us but equally important in the history of Christianity—St. Basil of Caesarea, St. Gregory of Nyssa, St. Gregory Nazianzus, St. John Chrysostom—give an idea of the incredible vitality of Christian culture at that moment in time. Of course, Christianity was still quite litigious, torn by theological disputes, full of heretical movements fighting against one another; nevertheless, Christian culture was increasingly setting the tone for the entire empire. Moreover, in 380, with the Edict of Thessalonica, the emperor Theodosius would decree that Catholic Christianity, in the form promulgated by the First Council of Nicaea in 325, was by law the sole, obligatory religion of all the empire's subjects. This would mark a drastic change of course from the tolerance that had been a feature of Constantine's edict of 313. Barely two years passed from the battle of Adrianople in 378 to the Edict of Thessalonica, and in a certain sense this codified repression on the part of the imperial government can be counted among the consequences of that disaster.

II

THE EMPIRE AND THE BARBARIANS

The Roman Empire in the fourth century, therefore, was not an empire in decline; and a proof of this assertion is the fact that the barbarians wanted to join it. One of the crucial dynamics in the history of late antiquity derives from the mass population movements that speakers of Romance languages, the modern languages descended from Latin, generally refer to as the *barbarian invasions.* German historians, who tend to see things from the newcomers' point of view rather than that of the local citizenry, prefer to talk of *Völkerwanderungen* (migrations of peoples). Considering what we now know about these mass movements, the German terminology more accurately describes them. Indeed contact between the empire and the barbarians, precisely in the form of immigration into Roman territory, had been going on for quite some time before 378, the year when the battle of Adrianople marked the beginning of a much more violent and dramatic period in Roman-barbarian relations. These tensions naturally focused on the borders. What, then, did the Romans see when they looked out beyond the guard posts along their frontiers? What did they know about the lands and peoples outside, lands and peoples whose existence the emperors never even officially recognized, given that imperial propaganda required them to pose as masters of the world?

Of course, they were well aware that other peoples and other countries existed beyond the borders of the empire. First and foremost was the powerful, civilized, and partly Hellenized Persian Empire to the east, Rome's only imperial rival, also known as the Sassanid or Sassanian Empire, from the name of the ruling dynasty at the time. The Persians had no wish to enter Roman territory and settle there; at most, they wanted to conquer the empire's rich eastern provinces. Here the clash was not between civilization and barbarians but between two civilizations that despised each other and had fought for centuries. These two powers were separated by the two great rivers of Mesopotamia, the Tigris and the Euphrates; sometimes the Romans advanced and established a bridgehead on the farther bank of the Tigris; at other times the Persians penetrated Roman territory even as far as Antioch on the Mediterranean Sea.

Elsewhere, however, no such fearful enemies threatened the imperial borders. To the south, along its Arabian and African boundaries, the empire was protected not by rivers but by deserts. The local peoples were nomads, and keeping them out would have been difficult; quite probably the Romans did not even try. In fact, the borders of the empire were not impassable barriers and the Romans a population under siege, obsessed with making sure no one got in. The nomads moved back and forth across the imperial frontiers, which served to keep them under observation, not to keep them out. When their raiding grew excessive, they could be taught a lesson; otherwise, the Romans entered into agreements with their chieftains and paid them well to escort caravans and protect the desert tracks. The empire had few problems living with the Bedouin and Berber nomads. In certain areas, especially in Africa, tribal leaders were granted Roman citizenship, received Roman names, and built themselves villas that were actually little fortresses; their men replaced the Roman frontier guards.

Some zealous Christians were bothered by this practice, because the barbarians were pagans who swore their service oaths upon their own gods, but the fact was that such accords guaranteed the security of the empire.

* * *

On Rome's northern borders, where the barbarians came from the cold, a different set of circumstances existed. Here the imperial frontiers were marked by two great rivers, the Rhine and the Danube, and Roman writers rejoiced that Nature—or Providence, if they were Christians—had placed those two bodies of water where they were, because they held the barbarians at bay. Exceptionally frigid winters, when the great rivers froze, and unusually torrid summers, when their water levels sank, were the seasons that the Romans most feared, because in such conditions those natural barriers were diminished, and the empire had to be on its guard. In fact, the most dangerous of all the barbarians the empire faced lived on the other sides of those two rivers, in a multitude of tribes that the Romans occasionally tried to inventory, classify, and describe; in reality, however, they knew and cared little about the outsiders, because the Romans recognized no value in diversity.

If anything about the barbarian hinterlands attracted the attention of Roman writers, it was the geographic variety to be found there. Besides, knowledge of such places was a necessary factor when deciding a political course or planning a military campaign. East of the Rhine and north of the Upper Danube lay Germania, a land of forests and swamps where the Romans had gotten their fingers burned more than once, starting back in the reign of Augustus Caesar, when three entire legions under the command of Quinctilius Varus were slaughtered by Germanic tribesmen in the battle of the Teutoburg Forest. The Romans no longer had any desire to occupy those lands, but they had been there in the past, even penetrating as far as the River Elbe; Germania was not an unknown country to them. And the Germans themselves, although a ferocious and dangerous enemy, were nevertheless familiar, almost domestic, ever since Tacitus had written his appropriately named *Germania*, a great ethnographic treatise ahead of its time. The Germans' martial abilities could even be transformed into an advantage for the empire: The Roman army was filled with immigrants from the Germanic tribes—excellent, loyal soldiers, all of whom made the military their career.

The Danube frontier was different. The Romans did not have a very good idea of what lay beyond it, especially in the lands around the mouth of the river, where it flows into the Black Sea; there was talk of immense steppes, extending far to the north, where no one had ever gone. Those steppes spread out across the Ukraine and lead directly to the plains of central Asia, the homeland of the nomads who for millennia flung themselves in waves upon the great, established civilizations, upon China and India as well as the Roman Empire. And these nomadic tribes, always on the point of boiling over, made the Danube frontier worrisome. Of course, among the nearest peoples, the Goths and the Sarmatians, the process of civilization had begun long since. They traded with the Romans and practiced a crude form of agriculture in addition to raising animals; but their nomadic traditions were still identifiable in the ease with which they could decide to move from one place to another en masse, with their families and their livestock, loading their household goods onto wagon trains and heading off in search of territory that would be more fertile or more secure.

The Germans on the far side of the Rhine caused comparatively less anxiety. They had been farmers forever; they lived in stable areas, each tribe in its own canton; they cultivated the soil; their leaders had already learned to construct fortified villas for themselves in the style of the great villas of the Roman countryside. Relations with the Germans could be managed. The steppe dwellers on the other side of the Danube struck much more fear into Roman hearts, because behind those peoples lay the Unknown.

* * *

Fear was certainly a key element in the Romans' attitude toward the barbarians, an ancestral fear evoked by the most dramatic moments in the history of ancient and republican Rome: the occupation of the city in 387 BC by Brennus and his Gauls, and the threat of the Cimbri and Teutoni, whom Marius defeated in 102 BC as they were about to flood into Italy. Roman writers returned to this obsession again and again: There are so many barbarians, too many, Germany produces wave upon wave of them, like the ocean, and new races are always being disgorged from the steppes. In the fourth century, this sort of rhetoric was actually quite familiar. It was kept alive by the orators whom the frontier provinces and the rich cities of Gaul, where the incursions of the Franks or the Alamanni posed a genuine threat, sent to Rome to supplicate the emperor. It was nourished by the news that came from the Danubian plains, where on more than one occasion the government was obliged to evacuate the inhabitants of the most exposed areas, withdraw garrisons, and relocate the refugees farther from the border, in order to escape the nomads' raids. It was revived by the lamentations coming in from the African frontier, where the great estate owners complained that the army was ineffectual, declared that it did not provide them with sufficient protection from barbarian forays, and threatened to arm their farmworkers and arrange for their own defense. But inside the imperial palace, the reasoning went differently. The ministers knew that the empire was capable of punishing the barbarians every time they raised their heads too high, and if Rome always had to settle for partial, temporary measures, that was merely a function of resources, of budgeting, of nonexistent funds and regiments below strength, and there was nothing to be afraid of.

Of course, the barbarians were warlike people, and they required frequent castigation, because they never learned their lesson. After a few years had passed since the last defeat, their courage would revive and they would enter imperial territory, attack farms, and carry off slaves and booty. The emperors would be obliged to intervene and organize punitive expeditions, which meant that then it was the Romans' turn to enter enemy territory, burn villages, massacre women and children, carry off livestock, and destroy harvests until the tribal chieftains came and begged for mercy on their knees. And then the same great estate owners and merchants who had complained about the lack of security derived huge profits from the captured slaves, from the compulsory tributes imposed on the barbarian tribes, from the livestock that the army brought back to the homeland and distributed to the people. Anyone who had seen his harvest destroyed and his slaves dispersed could request the army to assign him a gang of prisoners to work on his land for free. Meanwhile, recruiting officers scoured the encampments of the defeated and humiliated barbarians, selected the most robust young men, and carried them off; they would be branded, reeducated, taught discipline, and turned into Roman soldiers. The great estate owners, who were obligated to furnish the army with recruits chosen from among their farmers, were more than happy to pay a tax instead, seeing that the army was doing its recruiting on the other side of the frontier. The war against the barbarians was a business, like any other; all it required was proper management.

* * *

The Romans of the fourth century, in short, had an ambivalent attitude toward the barbarians. Everything they had learned from their ancestors inclined them to regard barbarians as beasts and not men, a force of nature capable only of destruction, and therefore to believe that it was necessary to exterminate them without mercy. But to those who considered the matter in the palaces of power, with revenue reports and regimental lists at hand, the barbarians were increasingly seen as something else: abundant, low-cost manpower, exactly what an empire obliged to maintain an enormous army for its own protection most needed. The more the government attempted to bring its military units to full strength by recruiting within the empire, the more it risked damaging agricultural production, displeasing the great proprietors, and—gravest consequence of all—reducing internal revenue. The bureaucrats who governed the empire and the large landowners who constituted the dominant class in every province found themselves in agreement: The barbarians were a potential resource that should not be wasted.

With this new perspective, the fourth-century Romans were able to perceive something that their forebears had never wanted to see: Very often, those groups of poor wretches who entered the empire clandestinely and survived illegally until they got captured in some roundup were only people on the run from hunger, from misery, from the violence of enemy tribes; people who knew no language except force, but who could be welcomed and put to work, given that there was never any shortage of work in the empire; people who, after they were defeated or captured, gladly accepted being put behind a plow or inducted into the imperial army. Once this realization occurred, its logical consequences followed: The imperial administration started getting ready to receive groups of barbarians, even sizable groups, and to settle them in the empire. Governmental departments arose, charged with overseeing this reception. They had previously served to relocate Roman refugees fleeing from devastated provinces or prisoners who had fallen into the hands of the barbarians and been subsequently liberated, but more and more often, the officials received orders to settle entire communities of immigrants in sparsely populated areas where manpower was needed, while jurists worked out the laws that bound those immigrants to the land and obligated them to pay taxes and to furnish their sons as conscripts to the army.

Before the battle of Adrianople, therefore, the barbarian invasions had already begun, but they were, for the most part, peaceful invasions carried out by submissive barbarians, who with their labor force contributed more than a little to the economic soundness of the Mediterranean world. As long as the imperial administration was capable of managing this immigration peacefully, with clear rules and conscientious oversight, the growing number of immigrants doesn't seem to have caused problems or repercussions of any kind. After all, the Roman Empire already was a multiethnic crucible of languages, races, and religions, and it was perfectly capable of absorbing massive immigration without becoming destabilized.

III

THE GOTHS AND ROME

On the battlefield at Adrianople, the Romans found themselves facing not so much an army of barbarian invaders as an entire people—the Goths—who had been seeking admission into the empire. The Goths were one of the major barbarian peoples; just one generation later, under their leader Alaric, they would go so far as to subject Rome itself, the capital of the world, to the famous sack of AD 410, a symbolic date in the history of the empire's collapse under the pressure of the invasions.

But who were the Goths, exactly? Today, we are accustomed to thinking of them as a Germanic people. We have a good knowledge of their language, and we know it belonged to the subfamily of Indo-European languages that specialists classify as Germanic. The Romans, however, did not and could not know this; in general, they had very little interest in barbarian tongues, and moreover they were lacking the knowledge of comparative linguistics they would have needed to arrive at certain conclusions.

The Goths, who were tall and blond or red-haired, physically resembled the Germans. The characteristics the two groups shared were all negative in Roman eyes; the dominant race in the Roman world, the race that believed it possessed a superior civilization and regarded all other races with contempt, was composed of short, dark Mediterranean types, and being tall and blond was a mark of inferiority, of poverty, of barbarism. In any case, no one then could have imagined that the Goths were Germans. For Roman writers, the Germans were simply the tribes that inhabited the forests and swamps of Germany. The Goths, on the other hand, lived in the eastern plains beyond the Danube, in the steppes that extended to the far-off Don River, and they resembled the other barbarians of the steppes: They were good horsemen, they were livestock breeders and shepherds as well as farmers, and they were a rootless people capable of moving easily from place to place.

The Romans were not completely wrong in making this classification, which, although they didn't know it, was an anthropological one. The steppe peoples were not compact ethnic groups; they were a multitude of tribes that came together, according to the circumstances, when some charismatic leader, some successful warrior, emerged among them. When we speak, for example, of the Huns—to mention another people who will play no small part in this story—it should be clear that only their original nucleus was formed by small, almond-eyed people with Mongolian features who raised livestock and spoke a Turkic language. At the height of their power, a few generations after Adrianople, they incorporated elements from every part of the steppes, including a large number of Goths who had become Huns. The two peoples mingled so thoroughly that Hunnish leaders spoke the language of the Goths fluently, and Attila, it should be noted, is a Gothic name.

In short, ethnic identity was in a continual state of negotiation, always liable to be reconstructed according to the movements of the various groups, however much Roman writers attempted to classify those groups as defined and unchanging. At the time of Adrianople, the clans that called themselves "Goths" had separated into different divisions, but these were not the familiar ones, the Visigoths and the Ostrogoths. The divisions bore much more ancient tribal names: The

Tervingi, the Greuthungi, and maybe others. Roman writers transcribed those names—they must have sounded quite odd in Latin—but the Romans were not interested in learning anything more about these people; whatever division they belonged to, they were all barbarians, poor illiterates living on the edge of starvation in their underdeveloped country.

* * *

An ignorant Roman, therefore, would have dismissed the Goths simply as barbarians, as an alien species foreign to his world. The only Goths he might have encountered—at the market, for example—would have been slaves, who came from all races, including the most exotic. But the intelligent ones Romanized themselves as fast as they could, trying to wipe out all trace of their ethnic identity, while the others had no future beyond a life of enervating labor on the plantations or in the mines.

However, the image of the barbarians as people radically foreign to the Roman world was a convenient but inaccurate simplification. The Goths had lived on the margins of the empire for centuries and through their contacts with Rome had begun to change their way of life. The Hungarian and Romanian archaeologists who excavated Gothic grave sites north of the Danube—the seventy-four tombs in the fourth-century necropolis at Sîntana de Mureş, for example—found that the dead had been buried with wheel-thrown earthenware objects, either of Roman manufacture or excellent imitations, and with buckles and jewelry made not only of bronze, silver, and amber, but also of hard stones and colored glass, which could have come only from Rome.

Gothic farmers and sheepherders had long been accustomed to seeing Roman traders, usually of Greek or Syrian origin, turn up in their villages. Thanks to these frequent contacts, the Goths' agricultural methods, although still primitive, may even have begun to improve. Their leaders were well aware that an extremely rich civilization, offering every sort of possibility, existed on the other side of the broad Danube. Crossing the river with a band of warriors in search of booty was an obvious and most dangerous temptation: The barbarians had learned that once they started to play that game, sooner or later, the Romans would react, and their punitive expeditions were appalling. However, the barbarians, who by dint of negotiating and trading with the Romans were becoming a little less barbaric, had also learned what high Roman officials were realizing: The empire needed mercenary soldiers, and it paid them well.

Rome, in fact, had thousands of miles of border to defend and powerful enemies to resist; the Roman army was the strongest in the world, but it was always hungry for manpower. However, the possibility of enrolling permanently in the Roman legions was not what chiefly attracted the attention of the Gothic chieftains and their warriors. It had long been customary for Rome to recruit foreigners, barbarians, to serve in its ranks. In such cases, the recruits would become Roman soldiers, abandoning family and country to begin a new life, and those who survived twenty-five years of service rarely wanted to return to a homeland with which they had almost nothing in common anymore. This trade-off suited many recruits who were disposed to do anything to escape a life of misery, but it was not a choice everyone wished to make. What really interested the trans-Danubian barbarians was the fact that the Romans, in addition to recruiting men for their regular units, were also enlisting short-term volunteers, mercenary troops engaged for a single campaign; and for this market, the Goths were the most available supply. It was especially convenient to sign them on for wars against the Persians, because the transfer from the Danube frontier to the Euphrates frontier was not difficult. Thus, whenever a Roman emperor planned a campaign against Persia, one of the first things he did was to contact the Gothic tribal leaders, offer them gifts and subsidies, and gain their consent to send some warrior troops to beef up the army gathering in Mesopotamia. One of our sources for these practices, the Greek rhetorician Libanius, observed that the system had another advantage: Since the majority of those mercenaries would wind up being killed, the barbarians could thus be more or less inconspicuously thinned out and Rome's borders made more secure.

* * *

During the course of the fourth century, before the battle of Adrianople, the leaders of the Goths had grown accustomed to making permanent agreements with the Roman Empire. In fact, the habit as well as the necessity of negotiating with the empire may have induced the Goths to organize their tribes into more numerous federations, which in turn resulted in the emergence of leaders who were no longer mere tribal leaders but princes, or "kinglets," as the Romans called them. The treaties agreed upon stipulated that the said leaders were to furnish the empire with warriors when necessary, and in return they would receive gifts, pensions, and even regular subsidies to feed their people. The Roman administration was quite efficient when it came to buying up grain, oil, and meat at low prices from taxpayers and then redistributing all these goods according to the prevailing political exigencies. The populations of the two capitals, Rome and Constantinople, owed the major part of their sustenance to such gratis distributions, which put a considerable strain on the imperial treasury. They were, however, politically indispensable, because in exchange for them the emperor received the assurance of favorable public opinion and avoided the popular discontent that so often proved fatal to improvident sovereigns.

The maintenance of the army was also largely due to the free distributions, which could take the place of the soldiers' monetary stipend. And therefore, when it became necessary to keep the barbarians happy, nothing was more natural than providing them, too, with subsidies in kind. Constantine had been the first to stipulate such agreements, and the Gothic people venerated his memory and his name, honoring him as a great emperor whom the Goths had been well content to obey, almost as if they were his subjects. Libanius made a related observation: After Constantine's death in 337, he remarked, the Danube border was peaceful, and his son Constantius II had nothing to fear from the Goths, who "treated our emperor as if he were theirs." The traditional image of the empire's fortified, impassable borders and of the threatening barbarian world in restless ferment beyond them was beginning to blur. The Goths were assuredly not subjects of the emperor—they paid no taxes, and no Roman officials governed them—but the regular enlistment of Gothic mercenaries and the flow of stipends and subsidies had brought about radical changes in the life and economy of the tribes. After the Gothic princes signed the treaties with Constantine, they had grown accustomed to stable, regular shipments of grain, carried across the Danube in Roman boats, for the maintenance of their people; and warriors used the gold they earned by fighting as mercenary soldiers to buy whatever they needed from Roman merchants. Without realizing it, the Goths had become dependent on the empire, so much so that they probably would not have been able to survive had the Romans, for whatever reason, suspended their payments.

* * *

The familiarity established between the Goths and the empire produced another far-reaching consequence: The barbarians began to convert to Christianity. We have very little information about the gods they adored before they discovered Christ. One reason for our ignorance is that the Goths seem to have maintained an impenetrable silence on the subject of their rites; nevertheless, we know that their divinities were represented, or incarnated, by wooden or stone idols and other sacred objects inscribed with runic characters. All these objects had an enormous ritual importance. Gothic leaders who desired to prevent their men from converting to Christianity compelled them to perform sacrifices before the tribal idol and to eat the flesh of the sacrificial animals; many centuries later, a Nordic ode still evoked the war of the Goths against the Huns, declaring that the Hunnish enemy wished to take possession of the object sacred to the Goths, "the radiant stone on the bank of the Dnieper."

Whenever a tribe was forced to relocate, its first concern was the transportation of its idols and the sacred objects attached to them, which were consigned to the care of priests and priestesses. The treasure of Pietroasa, discovered in Romania in 1837 and composed of twenty-four handmade objects—plates, cups, priestly ornaments—all made of solid gold and including no item of feminine jewelry or article of everyday use, probably represents the endowment of a temple or tribal sanctuary.

Christianity was first brought to the land of the idolatrous Goths by the large groups of Roman prisoners carried off from the Balkans and Asia Minor during the Gothic raids of the third century. These prisoners were rather quickly integrated into the lowest level of the Goths' tribal society, the level of slaves and the poorest peasants, and the Christians among them began to proselytize. After Constantine established regular relations with the Goths, Greek-speaking Gothic Christians appeared, who lived and studied for more or less extended periods of time inside the empire and then returned to their people to spread the new faith among them.

The most important of these educated Goths was named Ulfila, a fine Germanic name derived from the root *ulf*, "wolf," with the diminutive suffix *–la*, which is typical of the Gothic language. Ulfila, "Wolfy," was in fact an intellectual who studied in Constantinople and performed an extraordinary feat: He invented an alphabet for writing his native language and used his invention to translate the Bible from Greek into Gothic. Of Ulfila's translation, all that has survived to our day are parts of the New Testament—the famous *Codex Argenteus*, written on purple vellum in silver ink—but they are enough to give us a better knowledge of the Gothic tongue than of any other Germanic language spoken during the period of the invasions. Having been consecrated as a bishop, this Hellenized intellectual returned home to oversee the isolated Christian communities that already existed among his people. His preaching, along with that of many other missionaries from within the empire, resulted in a growing number of new conversions.

But what version of Christianity did Ulfila and the other educated Goths bring back with them? This was a crucial question, and the answer to it would continue to affect the destiny of the Gothic people for a long time after the battle of Adrianople. In fact, the Christians of that time were not yet in agreement about the definition of the Trinity, about Christ's nature, or about the relationship between the Father and the Son, and the faith was split into ferociously quarreling factions. In the end, the triumphant faction was the one that called itself "Catholic"—that is, "universal"—and "orthodox," in the sense that it promoted the "right faith," according to which, as Catholics who recite the Nicene Creed still say today, Christ was "begotten, not made" and "of the same substance as the Father." But a conflicting opinion was defended by the theologian Arius, for whom Christ had been created by God the Father and was therefore subordinate to him. In the fourth and fifth centuries, people might kill or be killed over such matters. In 325, at Nicaea, the theory propounded by Arius and his followers, the Arians, was condemned as heretical in a great council convoked and presided over by Emperor Constantine in person. Decades later, however, the Arian Church still had deep roots, especially in the eastern empire, and its missionaries were in the front ranks when it came to converting pagans. The bishop who consecrated Ulfila was Arian, not orthodox, and those Goths who heeded his preaching and that of his disciples converted to the new faith in its Arian profession.

Almost two centuries later, in the time of Theodoric and Justinian, this choice would create great problems for the Goths and put them on a collision course with the imperial government, but in Ulfila's day no one could have foreseen such difficulties, because the Arians were still very powerful in the empire, particularly in the East. Even some emperors were Arians, and they, disregarding the decisions of the Council of Nicaea, tended to favor the Arian episcopate in its often brutal competition with the bishops of the orthodox Nicene faction. Gothic converts to Christianity, on the other hand, had problems with their own countrymen, because many tribal leaders were hostile to the new religion. There were rumors of repeated persecutions beyond the Danube and of a great number of Gothic martyrs stoned, burned, or drowned by order of their own chieftains; in the Roman Empire, by contrast, the persecutions of Christians had long since come to an end. By the last quarter of the fourth century, therefore, the Goths were fully engaged in the difficult, contested process of conversion to Christianity, a fact that adds yet another dramatic element to a story already quite dramatic in its own right.

* * *

After Constantine the Great concluded a treaty with their leaders in 332, the Goths maintained excellent relations with the Roman Empire for an extended period. Things deteriorated quite rapidly, however, after Constantine's dynasty came to an end and the imperial throne was occupied by new men toward whom the Goths felt no sense of obligation. In 364, the Roman army—which by this time usually appointed emperors without even asking the opinion of the Senate—decided, after much discussion, to acclaim one of its generals, Valentinian, as the new ruler of the empire. Shortly after assuming the diadem, Valentinian chose to name a colleague and divide the empire into two parts, eastern and western. Such a procedure was common enough, because the empire was immense, and as we've already seen, when the emperor was far away, rebellions could break out in the provinces or a general could attempt to usurp the imperial throne. Therefore, it was reasonable to have two or even three emperors, each of them with a more limited area to control. At the time of his acclamation, Valentinian was fighting against the Germans along the Rhine; he decided to keep the western empire under his command and appointed his brother Valens emperor in the East.

Valens would become one of the leading figures—perhaps the tragic protagonist—in the story of the battle of Adrianople. He and his brother were two very different personalities. Valentinian was a tough soldier, an energetic, victorious general, and a great organizer, who taught the barbarians some unforgettable lessons and successfully stabilized the western frontiers. He was a provincial from a modest family and, like many military men, probably not very cultivated; but he had a genius for politics, good instincts, and a natural tendency to do the right thing. For example, in an empire lacerated by religious controversies, Valentinian was able to impose a truce and compel substantial tolerance, so that pagans, Christians, and Arian Christians were obliged to coexist without slaughtering one another. In comparison to him, Valens seemed a less remarkable person; he was the younger brother, and he had always lived to some extent in Valentinian's shadow.

When Valentinian named him emperor in the East, Valens was thirty-six years old. On coins, he was portrayed as a man inclined toward corpulence, with a thick neck and already a hint of a double chin. The best chronicler of the time, Ammianus Marcellinus, asserted that Valens had slightly bowed legs, a paunch, and one bad eye, although you had to be close to him to notice it. He was, however, a decent man, and he set to work with goodwill, resolved not to cut a poor figure in his brother's eyes. Rather condescendingly, Ammianus further observed that Valens was uneducated and somewhat uncouth, but he worked hard to combat corruption and tried to reduce taxes, and in the beginning of his reign he established a good reputation. He also invested in public works, such as the great aqueduct (called, naturally, the Valens aqueduct) that supplied Constantinople with water, a large section of which still stands in Istanbul today.

Despite all his efforts, however, Valens's subjects did not like him.

Perhaps the reason for his unpopularity lay in a character trait that distinguished him from his brother: Valens was a religious fanatic. He was a Christian, but of the Arian variety, and his policies served to exacerbate religious conflicts instead of settling them. He persecuted Catholics, using his authority to close their churches, and sent bishops who tried to resist into exile. In the latter half of the fourth century, when Christian society was on the verge of splitting apart over religious questions, such policies were anything but prudent, and Valens suffered the consequences. Discontent spread among his Catholic subjects, and tensions ran so high in some large cities like Alexandria that Valens was forced to rescind the measures he had taken and recall the exiled bishops. None of this served to strengthen his position, and had Valens been required to stand for election, he would have been soundly beaten. But Roman emperors were appointed for life, and the only way to get rid of them was to kill them; and so, though his image had been tarnished by the religious conflicts he had been unable to manage, Valens remained in power.

The other source of difficulty for Valens, right from the beginning of his reign, had been the Goths. When the news spread that Valentinian had named his brother emperor in the East, a general named Procopius, who was in Constantinople at the time, rose in revolt and had himself proclaimed emperor by his troops. Procopius had two good cards to play: He controlled the capital, and he was related to the family of Constantine the Great. In their steppes beyond the Danube, the Gothic leaders learned about what was happening and decided that their people were not bound by treaty to the Roman Empire, but to Constantine and his family. Clearly, there was little room in their worldview for any abstract idea of the state, but they understood personal ties perfectly. Unfortunately for them, however, they made the wrong choice: They sent troops of warriors to support Procopius, but by the time they arrived, the usurper had already been defeated and killed, and Valens was in power. The victorious emperor threw all the barbarian troops into prison and entered into negotiations with the Gothic leaders for the return of their men. But the negotiations broke down, and Valens, who was endowed with little patience to begin with, lost what he had and sold all the Gothic soldiers into slavery.

At this point, the old treaty between the Goths and the empire had been obliterated, and Valens quickly decided to settle matters in his own way. He crossed the Danube with his army and began a meticulous devastation of the countryside in order to teach the barbarians to stay where they belonged. No major battles were fought, but Valens's scorched-earth policy worked, among other reasons because up to that moment the Goths had been accustomed to counting on the subsidies paid by the Romans, on their regular supplies of free grain, and on the possibility of doing business with merchants from the empire. With all these benefits at a sudden stop, the Goths were literally at risk of starving to death. In the end, their leaders came to Valens on their knees and begged him to make peace.

* * *

We do not know the text of the treaty that Valens imposed on the Goths in AD 369 after defeating them and reducing them to hunger, but we do have an exceptional piece of evidence that demonstrates what the imperial propagandists wanted the emperor's subjects to believe about the government's Gothic policy. It is a speech delivered in the presence of the emperor by the Greek rhetorician Themistius, one of the most influential political men in Constantinople, who spoke in praise of Valens for having made peace. We may call the ideology reflected in this speech progressive and humanist; it was a way of thinking quite common at the time in the ruling circles of the empire, and a counterpoint to the calculated cruelty with which Roman troops conducted their operations in enemy territory.

Like almost every politician in the empire, Themistius was convinced that the barbarians could be civilized—it was just a question of commitment—and that one day they, too, could become the emperor's useful subjects, which in the language of the day chiefly meant reliable taxpayers. Therefore Themistius praised Valens, who could have annihilated the Goths but instead chose to spare them, and then the rhetorician made the following extraordinary comparison: We worry so much, he said, about preserving animal species, we're worried that elephants may disappear from Libya, lions from Thessaly, and hippopotamuses from the Nile; therefore we should rejoice that "a race of men, yes, barbarians, as some will say, but men" has been saved from extermination.

One would not imagine that these environmental considerations, this concern for Libyan elephants and Nile hippopotamuses, were current among the Hellenized elite of the Roman Empire, but what is most interesting in the speech is the humanitarian implication that the empire, while aspiring to dominate the world, had to also dedicate itself to the goal of civilizing the barbarians. Genocide was dismissed as a losing option unworthy of a great civilization. One can safely assume that more than one general considered the matter differently in private, but such opinions could no longer be publicly espoused, and not only because the empire had become Christian. The influence of the clergy is not sufficient to explain the penetration of these humanitarian ideals into the thought of such intellectuals as Themistius or Libanius, who were pagans. The fact is that the ideology of the empire was being based more and more openly upon the strength of its attraction for all humanity; indeed, the pressure of the barbarians on the borders of the empire served to confirm this view and required emperors to display goodwill toward "those people who have never had the opportunity to be Romans," to cite another rhetorician of the time. The idea that integration into the empire was to be encouraged became the order of the day, and the emperors, in their laws, expressed their satisfaction on this point, because "many people of foreign origin have come into our empire, following the dream of Roman felicity."

Therefore, when Themistius praised Valens for having made peace with the Goths instead of slaughtering the lot of them, he represented the humanitarian and universalistic ideology typical of the late Roman Empire. One can debate whether the Romans really believed in such notions or whether they were only a cover for a thoroughly unscrupulous imperialism; the Roman Empire was not alone in offering discrepancies between political speeches full of high-sounding principles and the brutality of political praxis. But in order to understand the climate that fostered the battle of Adrianople, those speeches must be kept firmly in mind, those elegantly constructed Greek phrases that echoed in the halls of the imperial palace and the Senate in Constantinople. Today, Themistius said in his oration, the Roman emperor is the father not only of a people but of all humanity; his task is indeed to mortify the insolence of the barbarians, but also to protect and guide them paternally until they may become "part of the empire."

The actual ways by which the Goths could become part of the empire after the peace of 369 reflected the distance that lay between fine speeches and reality. Because Valens planned to make war on the Persians, he needed mercenary soldiers; therefore, as had always been done in the past, he began to enlist Gothic troops and to transfer them to the Mesopotamian border country to wait until a sufficient force had been gathered and the campaign could begin. So the empire certainly did have room for the Goths, but as a very particular kind of manpower, as what we would call "cannon fodder" today.

Valens also made room for them in another, even more twisted way. After his punitive expeditions, the land of the Goths on the far side of the Danube was devastated, and the new treaty was less favorable to them than the one with Constantine had been. As part of a policy of sanctions designed to punish the Goths for having rebelled and to teach them obedience in the future, the Romans suspended their subsidies and grain provisions. Even the possibilities of engaging in commerce with Roman traders, a commerce that had played such an important role in satisfying the Gothic princes' need for luxury and in saving their people from starvation in case of shortages, became more restricted than they had been in the past. In the land of the Goths, therefore, the standard of living declined, just as it does in any poor country targeted by commercial sanctions. This was an ideal situation for slave merchants, who had no difficulty finding ruined families willing to sell a son or a daughter. Although such a practice seems unthinkable to us, it arose fairly often in societies accustomed to slavery. A great wave of Gothic slaves surged into the empire, so many that the market was flooded and prices collapsed. In the words of another contemporary, Synesius, who owned a great estate in Africa and later became a Christian bishop, "Any family that is even moderately well-off has a Gothic slave; in every home, there is a Goth preparing the table, tending the oven, carrying the amphora; and among the slaves who serve as escorts outside the home, those who bear folding stools on their backs so their masters can sit down along the way are all Goths."

IV

THE EMERGENCY OF 376

Such was the situation in the fall of 376, when some terribly disturbing news spread among the citizens of the Roman Empire. The news was not official, it was unconfirmed, and no one knew who had first disseminated it; but it traveled from mouth to mouth, and people were frightened. The reports stated that the barbarians of the North had begun to move; that some unknown cataclysm had driven entire populations from their homes along the whole course of the Danube, all the way to the delta and the Black Sea; and that those populations were wandering menacingly just beyond the imperial borders. In the great cities of the Balkans and the Middle East, such information was conveyed in whispers in the marketplaces and the baths, because circulating subversive rumors was a capital crime in the Roman Empire. Naturally, the government neither denied nor confirmed the rumors—the emperor habitually acted in secret and responded to public opinion only when it suited him—but this very fact increased the people's anxiety. As a rule, the diffusion of news was generally well controlled by official propaganda, and when the northern barbarians were mentioned, it was only to announce another victory over them; the public learned about a war along the Danube frontier only when the emperor declared that combat had ended with the inevitable victory. The current rumors, by contrast, were vague and inconclusive. People did not know what to think and were thus anxious.

In the imperial palace, however, rather more was known. Emperor Valens was at that moment in Syria, in the city of Antioch, some twelve hundred miles from the Danube frontier, busily preparing for war against the Persians. News, including what was brought posthaste by official couriers changing horses at every stage along the route, took weeks to reach him, an example of how the vastness of the empire and the practical difficulty of governing it had led to the practice of dividing the imperial power. When, at last, news arrived, the emperor and his advisers determined that the situation on the northern frontier was much less troubling than the common horde believed it to be. Of course, not a thought was given to informing and reassuring public opinion, for the emperor would never have felt he owed his subjects an accounting. But in the secrecy of the *consistorium* (the ministers' confidential meeting in the presence of the emperor), Valens and his counselors, the eunuchs who governed the imperial palace and the generals of the imperial guard, were not worried about a thing.

* * *

What had happened to set the northern barbarians in motion? What was the cataclysm that had driven them from their homes and carried them, like a flood tide, to the banks of the Danube? The news that reached Antioch had been detailed enough to allow the emperor to make a shrewd guess concerning its background. A new people had appeared in the steppes of Asia, a race so little known that its name sent Roman officials and generals to the imperial library in search of further information. But the search proved futile: The ancient historians had nothing useful to say about the new race. These people were the Huns, with whom the Romans would become all too familiar over the course of the next hundred years; up to this point, however, the little that was known about them was anything but reassuring. It was reported that they had the repulsive habit of using knives to slash the cheeks of their barely newborn infants, leaving scars that remained visible for a lifetime. A modern anthropologist would immediately recognize the ritual scarring or tattooing practiced by many primitive peoples, a language written on the body and heavy with sacred significance and affirmations of identity. But the Romans were not anthropologists, and they tried to rationalize the practice in question. The explanation for it, according to them, was that the Huns didn't like facial hair, and so they slashed their male infants' cheeks to prevent their beards from growing.

Equally repellent was another of their customs, one that became legendary and remains well known to this day: The Huns, it was said, nourished themselves with raw meat, which they warmed "between their thighs and the backs of their horses," according to Ammianus Marcellinus, who was the first to tell this tale. But the Huns' most significant characteristic was that they were genuine nomads of the Asian steppes, not simply people who possessed little and relocated easily, like the Goths, but pure, dyed-in-the-wool nomads who couldn't enter a walled house without a sensation of fear and revulsion, as though they were entering a tomb. As for themselves, they knew no other habitations but wagons and tents, and in practice they lived on horseback. In Ammianus's account of the Huns can be seen all the consternation of the sedentary man who identifies civilization with cities and agriculture and all the dismay of the Roman for whom a man's identity—and this way of thinking was utterly typical of the ancient mentality—depends on his place of origin. Thus the nomadic raisers of livestock represented an absolutely incomprehensible way of life. "They are like fugitives," Ammianus said, "taking along with them the wagons in which they live. In these wagons, their wives weave their horrible garments, lie with their husbands, give birth to their children, and rear them until they reach puberty. If asked, none of them could say from whence he came, as he was conceived elsewhere, born far away, and raised farther away than that." One could barely call such people human, and understanding them was impossible because their values were too different, and moreover, the Huns seemed to the Romans to have no value at all, with the exception of their avidity for gold. "Like beasts without reason," Ammianus concluded, "they make no distinction between right and wrong."

* * *

The Huns' nomadic way of life, which rendered them so incomprehensible to the Roman mind, also made them fearful enemies, capable of moving at high speed, appearing by surprise where no one expected them, and giving or refusing battle as they pleased. Huns fought on horseback, using nooses of plaited cloth to immobilize their adversaries and flinging javelins with sharp bone tips. (Ammianus, our source for this information, was pleased to portray the Huns as primitives; in their tombs, however, and in the skeletons of their enemies, archaeologists have in fact discovered excellently fashioned iron arrowheads.) The Huns, in short, were the type of mobile, treacherous enemy whom the Romans had always distrusted and with whom they had always felt ill at ease. In Valens's palace, therefore, no one was astonished when news came that the Goths, terrorized by the appearance of the Huns in their remoter territories, had been unable to stand against them: The Huns had crossed one river after another, the Don, the Dnieper, the Dniester, and wherever they passed, they massacred everyone they found, men, women, and children, in such a ferocious and systematic way that one ancient author described the events almost as a genocide.

The Goths did not know any more about the origin and nature of the Huns than the Romans did, and yet a legend, told and retold in their long night watches, soon began to spread among them, a legend that reveals a great deal about the terror the nomads had struck into Gothic hearts. According to this tale—which was still being recounted two centuries later—in the distant past a Gothic king named Filimer had discovered witches (*haliurunnae* in Gothic) among his people and cast them out. Driven from the tribe and compelled to wander the vast reaches of the steppes, the witches had coupled with the evil spirits that inhabited those deserted places, and from these monstrous couplings had sprung an equally monstrous, half-human race: the dreaded Huns.

Faced with relentless pressure from this terrifying enemy—extremely mobile squadrons of Hunnish raiders on horseback attacked Gothic villages, generally at dawn, and took no prisoners, except perhaps for some young women they carried off into slavery—the panicked Gothic populations, along with their surviving livestock, took to flight: They loaded their household goods on wagons, formed convoys, and started moving south. Also a warlike people, the Goths made more than one attempt to resist, but every time they took on the Huns in a pitched battle, the results were disastrous. One after another, the Gothic princes were defeated, and their followers joined the throngs of refugees. Finally, all this mass of fleeing people, worn out from hunger and hardships after wandering for months, had arrived and made camp on the banks of the Danube, across the river from the Roman guard posts.

Fortunately, the Huns were still very far off and loaded down with an immense freight of booty, so that they probably wouldn't have advanced as far as the river. But all the country of the Goths was ravaged and reduced to wilderness, the fields unsown, the houses abandoned or burned. The refugees had neither the possibility nor the desire to go back to their accursed land, where the best they could hope for was to die of hunger. Beyond the Danube, they knew, was a huge empire, rich and civilized, where it was easy to find work; and so they asked for permission to enter. This was how the Gothic leaders explained their situation to the Roman officials who came to their makeshift camps, where thousands of refugees were packed together, to inquire as to their intentions; and this was the report that landed, a few weeks later, on Valens's desk in far-off Antioch. The officers who commanded the guard posts had submitted the report to the military governors of the frontier provinces, and they in turn had forwarded it to the emperor, with an urgent request for instructions: What were they to do with all these people?

* * *

We do not have a record of any of the discussions held by Valens and his counselors as they tried to decide how to respond to the Gothic refugees' request to be received into the empire. We have only Ammianus Marcellinus's reconstruction of such a discussion and should not place too much faith in it. Ammianus was not present in the *consistorium*, and since he was writing several years later, after everything had come to a very bad end, he was certainly not an objective witness. But the arguments that, in his account, were employed in the discussion and that in the end persuaded the emperor to make a decision appear quite credible, because they correspond perfectly to what was by then a well-established political practice. Everyone knew the empire needed manpower. All across its lands, entire provinces were depopulated or had actually become wasteland, especially those where inferior soil and a crushing tax burden made the land not worth cultivating. The state itself possessed vast tracts of real estate, but often it did not have sufficient manpower to cultivate its lands and was forced to lease them at bargain prices to entrepreneurs who profited from them.

The Goths, although barbarians, were nevertheless farmers, accustomed to working the fields. When the Gothic leaders requested land in Thrace, that they might settle their followers there and live in peace, the Romans found themselves with several options for granting their supplication. They could assign state lands, including property abandoned or confiscated, directly to the Gothic leaders, giving them the land outright or granting them leases in perpetuity, on very favorable terms; in either case, the leaders would see to distributing the lands among their people. Or the Romans could settle Gothic families directly on the large estates as tenant farmers. For some time, Roman law had been elaborating the status of the tenant farmer; personally he was a free man, not a slave, but he was legally obligated to remain on the land and cultivate it. Such a farmer would later receive the name of "serf," which is usually and erroneously associated only with the medieval period; in reality, however, the serf was a legal entity typical of the late Roman Empire. This solution was not as advantageous to the refugees as the others, but as people dying of hunger, they were in no position to stipulate conditions.

Finally, the emperor had to take into account another, even more pressing necessity: conscripts for the army. Receiving the Goths into the empire was equivalent to enlarging the pool of potential recruits with a multitude of young men in the prime of life and inured to combat; and every Goth enrolled in an imperial regiment would mean that a native recruit could, for a price, obtain an exemption. There were evident advantages for all concerned: for the army, for the treasury, but also for public opinion in the provinces, where conscription was barely tolerated, as nobody liked removing tenant farmers from the fields and sending them to serve the emperor. The emperor's counselors thus saw nothing dangerous in the throng of barbarians massing along the frontier; on the contrary, they had apparently been sent there by Valens's good fortune.

* * *

The Goths had already been camped on the bank of the Danube for a long time, under an incessant rain that made the river swell before their eyes, when finally the emperor's orders arrived from Antioch. Valens's response was what the Gothic princes had hoped: The refugees were to be received peacefully. On the other side of the river, humanitarian assistance was awaiting them, and then, down the road, the prospect of housing and work. As their first order of business, the officials sent by the emperor had precise instructions to arrange for the ferrying of the entire Gothic multitude to the Roman side of the Danube. This was necessary because no bridges spanned the river; along all its immense course, only a single bridge had ever existed, a stone structure built some fifty years previously by order of Constantine, for the precise purpose of demonstrating to the Goths the length of his reach and the ease with which, should the barbarians misbehave, his legions could enter their country. But the bridge had already fallen into ruin, and therefore water transport had to be arranged. This was another of the things that the Roman administrators, capitalizing on the skills of the army, knew how to do well. They confiscated fishing vessels up and down the river, saw to the building of makeshift rafts and pontoons, and began ferrying operations.

The river crossing continued for several days and perhaps even for several weeks, so great was the barbarian multitude. When Ammianus Marcellinus reflected upon this exercise, he was overcome with rage at the idea that such great efforts were made to help a group of people enter the empire who would in the end reveal themselves to be its mortal enemies. His language is revealing: As far as he was concerned, the Goths were a *plebs truculenta*, a mob of dangerous ruffians; and, he continued, "assiduous care was taken to insure that no one was left behind, not one of those who would later overthrow the Roman state, not even if they were mortally ill." Incessantly, day and night, men, women, children, and horses were ferried across the river in every sort of vessel and even in hollowed-out tree trunks. This last detail serves, among other things, to remind us of the Roman world's fundamental technical backwardness, which contrasts so starkly with its organizational capacity and its intellectual refinement.

Among the throng awaiting their turn on the far bank, in constant fear that the Huns might at any moment appear at their backs, tension must have run exceedingly high, and as in all humanitarian operations undertaken in emergency situations, there was no lack of tragic mishaps. The Danube is in any case a dangerous river, and at that moment it was swollen by the torrential rains. Many boats capsized, many people, in their desperation, tried to swim across, and we have no record of how many drowned. Nevertheless, the Goths continued to disembark, day and night. At desks set up along the riverbank, the officials charged with receiving the barbarians were waiting with orders to write down every one of their names; the administration wanted to have a complete list in hand in order to calculate the number of immigrants who would have to be settled. But the ferrying operations were carried out amid such confusion, and so many people crossed in makeshift craft of their own devising, that in the end the imperial agents lost count of the new arrivals and stopped even trying to arrive at a tally.

* * *

In addition to Ammianus Marcellinus's pages on the Goths' Danube crossing, another chronicle of these events has survived, written in Greek by a historian named Eunapius. Only fragments of his work remain, but luckily one of them contains this very episode. His account is quite similar in substance to that of Ammianus; and as they were very different authors unknown to each other, it permits us to conclude that events must have occurred more or less as the two writers described them. Eunapius added an artful description of the Gothic warriors, standing on the bank of the Danube and stretching out their arms toward the Roman side as they recounted the tragedy of their people, begging to be received, and pledging themselves to serve in the Roman army. As it is unlikely that the supplicants could have made themselves heard from one bank of the Danube to the other, a distance of more than a mile and with the great river in flood between them, we may imagine that Eunapius made up this detail out of whole cloth; but he did not include it by chance. In the version set down by Eunapius, in fact, the imperial government's decision to admit the refugees was based solely on its desire to increase the size of the army, and for this reason Valens ordered that only males, duly disarmed, be allowed to cross the river into Roman territory.

Taken literally, Eunapius's version is unlikely, if for no other reason than that the Goths would never have accepted such conditions. But the Greek historian calls attention to another aspect of the matter, one that allows a better understanding of Valens's motivations. In the previous year, Valentinian, the older of the two emperors, had died, leaving the power in the West to his two sons, Gratian and Valentinian II. The succession of an emperor was a delicate moment in which anything, including rebellions or attempts at usurpation, could happen. Valens had kept up good relations with his brother, but he surely could not have trusted nephews in the same way, and therefore at such a time he would have been particularly attracted by the opportunity to enlist in his army a large number of Gothic warriors.

Another detail, related by Eunapius with indignation, is similarly credible. While everyone was still waiting for the emperor's response, some groups of Goths, the most audacious and enterprising, tried to cross the river clandestinely, but Roman patrols intercepted and mercilessly destroyed them. When Valens's emissaries arrived with the news that the Goths were not to be considered as enemies but rather as a precious resource, the officials who had suppressed the barbarians' attempts at clandestine immigration were removed from their duties and placed under investigation. Eunapius was furious as he recounted this episode, but he very well understood what was going on behind the scenes: The politicians, for motives of their own, had decided to follow a soft line with regard to these immigrants, and they had no intention of allowing the military to address the problem in its own characteristic fashion.

* * *

Eunapius's account confirms that the delivery of the Gothic refugees to the Roman bank of the Danube was carried out in the most chaotic conditions, and it adds other revealing details concerning the widespread lawlessness and the abuses committed by the Roman government officials and military officers who oversaw the operation. The order was to have the adolescent males, who would be held as hostages, cross first, followed by the adult males, but only after they were disarmed. However, corruption was so rampant that many Goths who paid bribes were able to cross with their families as well as their weapons. Many other refugees, especially women and little boys, were transported across the river illegally by government officials and army officers who planned to carry the newcomers home as their own personal slaves. "Simply put," Eunapius said, "they had all decided to fill their houses with domestics and their land with shepherds and to exploit the situation in order to satisfy their every desire." One can easily imagine that an operation that could be called, in theory, humanitarian, an operation assigned to corrupt bureaucrats and brutal soldiers and conducted on a remote frontier well out of the government's sight, without means of mass communication capable of keeping tabs on events and without any obligation to consult public opinion, might really have been handled in such a disturbing way.

But in the meantime, day after day, the refugees kept arriving on the Roman bank of the Danube, where they camped in numbers so much greater than anticipated that no one had a very clear idea of what to do with them. The emperor's orders specified that the immigrants were to be transferred to sparsely populated regions and given enough cultivable land to sustain themselves; but this, obviously, was a process that would require some time, and in fact the orders from Antioch expressly commanded the local authorities to provide rations for all those people during this intermediate stage. And so, day after day, a huge refugee camp expanded along the riverbank, guarded by Roman soldiers and subsisting on the rations distributed by the Roman army. Indeed the throngs of refugees continued to arrive, in ever increasing numbers, on the opposite bank. The news that the border was open and that the Romans themselves were ferrying immigrants over to their side of the river had spread rapidly, and everyone wanted to take advantage of the opportunity. Eventually, however, the authorities grew alarmed. When new tribal chieftains at the head of well-organized convoys presented themselves at the frontier and made an explicit appeal for the humanitarian assistance they hoped to receive, they were told that there was no more room. And so a growing multitude was encamped on the northern side of the river as well. Restless and malcontent from the start, these people became more and more openly hostile to the incomprehensible empire that had so abruptly denied them access. The Roman boats, having suspended their ferrying activities, patrolled the river to prevent clandestine landings.

* * *

The situation was also deteriorating for the immigrants who had already been admitted, mostly because of the frightening inadequacy of the arrangements made to receive them. The refugee camps were overcrowded, hygienic conditions were disastrous, and the rations furnished by the army were barely sufficient to stave off starvation. Officials should have started marching the immigrants to the interior of the empire, as the imperial instructions required, but the Roman generals in command—Duke Maximus, at the head of the frontier troops, and Count Lupicinus, the military governor of Thrace—were in no hurry. The two of them had quickly realized that great potential profit lay in the rations they were supposed to furnish to the refugees. Corruption was endemic in the Roman Empire, and the entire system of contracts and supplies for the army had always offered unlimited opportunities for criminal gain.

There was so much money to be made from the provisions intended for the Gothic refugees that the generals naturally tried to make the scam last longer. If the meager supplies that actually reached the refugee camps, and then only because of bribes, proved insufficient to nourish all the immigrants, the generals stood to gain even more, because on the black market they could always sell those desperate people the food they should have received for free. Eventually, living conditions in the camps reached such extremes that the Goths were prepared to sell their children in exchange for a little bad wine and vile bread; the Romans even went so far as to sell the Goths dogs, which they bought in order to feed themselves.

In the end, the enterprise became unmanageable. Maximus and Lupicinus began to fear that they would be denounced; the Gothic leaders openly protested because the promised supplies never came, and the situation grew more dangerous with each passing day. Finally, Lupicinus decided to carry out the emperor's orders and set the refugees moving toward the interior of the empire, where the administration was hastily preparing the areas designated for settlement. The leading Goths, who despite everything still believed that the promises made to them would be kept, ordered their people to ready their wagons, and the convoy began to move. All available military units were called in to escort the Goths on their way, because they were in such a state of mind that the authorities feared incidents; as for the civilian population, it was not at all favorably disposed toward this multitude of barbarians passing through their country. In fact, the situation was already out of control, although Valens, still in Antioch, had no idea what was happening, and probably even Maximus and Lupicinus failed to realize how bad things were. Escorting the barbarian convoy to the interior would require a march of several weeks, and to this end, the guard posts along the river had been stripped of their garrisons and the military boats obliged to shut down their patrolling operations. But an enormous throng of refugees remained on the other bank of the Danube, people who had arrived too late to be able to cross, who had been refused admission, and who had stayed near the river, living in camps and filled with resentment. As soon as the soldiers withdrew, this mass of Goths started crossing the river illegally on makeshift rafts and setting up new camps in Roman territory without asking anyone's permission.

* * *

The transfer of the Gothic refugees across the Roman province of Thrace began in an atmosphere thick with tension. The barbarians numbered tens of thousands, an immense multitude of refugees, some of them civilians, but some armed warriors. Because of the promises they had been given, all of them were filled with anticipation, but they were also exasperated at the treatment they had received thus far, and their suspicions were aroused by the extraordinary security measures put in place by the Roman authorities. The soldiers, who escorted them with the utmost vigilance, were also nervous and suspicious, in large part because they were afraid there would not be enough of them to withstand the barbarians should they stage a mass revolt. One of the Gothic tribal chiefs, Fritigern, had by this time acquired the status of leader of the entire multitude of refugees; according to Ammianus, Fritigern was well aware of the gathering tensions, he was informed that other leaders and their people had crossed the river illegally, and he slowed the march as much as he could, so that in case of difficulty the illegals could join his forces and make common cause.

Whether or not Fritigern did it deliberately, the progress of the convoy, with all those families piled into some two or three thousand ox-drawn wagons, and with all the attendant problems of provision, must necessarily have been slow and difficult. After a few days, however, the vanguard drew within sight of the walls of a large city, Marcianople, now Devnja in present-day Bulgaria. This was the first major urban center that many of the Goths had ever seen, and it lay in the middle of a fertile region filled with fields and pastures for livestock. Perhaps the refugees thought they had finally arrived in the area where, in accordance with the emperor's orders, they were to be granted houses and land; in any case, they were hungry and worn down after the privations of the march, and they expected at least to be accommodated in the city and to receive a distribution of rations, as they had been promised.

In fact, however, nothing was ready for them in Marcianople. The local authorities had made no preparations whatsoever, hoping only that the throng of refugees would get back on the road as soon as possible, and the citizens, terrified of the barbarians, wanted nothing to do with them. The Goths believed they had become subjects of the emperor and were genuinely ready to obey orders, but they were dying of hunger; and when they requested permission at least to enter the city and buy food, the inhabitants prevented the opening of the gates. The infuriated Goths tried to force their way in, the soldiers of the escort intervened, the first clashes broke out, and then what the Roman generals should have known from the beginning became all too clear: There were not enough soldiers to hold the great multitude of barbarians at bay. The Roman troops were overcome, and the Goths, who at this point could only have expected the worst, stripped the bodies of their fallen adversaries, donned their armor, and took up their weapons.

* * *

While the first incidents were taking place outside the walls of Marcianople, Count Lupicinus, the highest Roman authority in the province and personally responsible for the transfer of the immigrants, was at a banquet inside the city with some of the Gothic tribal chiefs, among them Fritigern. Whether or not Lupicinus, in addition to being corrupt, was so thoroughly incompetent that he did not realize the situation was coming to a head is not known. In a certain sense, there was nothing odd about such a banquet; the Gothic leaders were there with the authorization of the emperor, and Lupicinus would have had to work closely with them in transferring their people and settling them in their new lands. This collaboration at the top between the Roman authorities and the barbarian princes was indispensable for the success of the operation, which had turned into the reception of immigrants on the largest scale ever attempted by an imperial administration. But Lupicinus may also have counted from the start on the halt at Marcianople as his opportunity, if there were any trouble, to rid himself of the barbarian leaders, in the hope that eliminating them would cause their followers to disperse. In any case, what ensued is one of those ugly stories that have given the period of the later empire its murky reputation for cruelty and immorality.

While Lupicinus and the tribal leaders feasted, the Goths outside the city rebelled and started killing the soldiers who were trying to reduce them to obedience. Ammianus Marcellinus, our only source for this episode, draws a memorable portrait of Lupicinus at the moment when someone comes into the banquet room and informs him of what is happening: The count, according to Ammianus, "had been reclining for a long time at an extravagantly laden table, surrounded by noisy entertainments, and he was heavy with wine and sleep." Nevertheless, he reacted quickly, and while he continued drinking with the Gothic leaders, his men, in the corridors of the palace, silently dispatched all the guards the Goths had brought with them. However, Lupicinus failed to seize the favorable moment, or perhaps he simply couldn't find the courage to have the Gothic princes' throats cut, too. The Goths outside the walls, realizing that their leaders had not returned, started rioting even more tumultuously and made a concerted attempt to enter the city by force; whereupon Lupicinus lost his head. Fritigern and the others, who must also have been affected by their prolonged drinking, finally noticed that something was amiss, approached Lupicinus, and, dissembling their concern, told him that there had been a mistake. Surely, they said, their men outside must believe that something had happened to their leaders. To avert a disaster, Fritigern declared, it was absolutely necessary for him and the others to go out and show themselves; once their people saw them unharmed, they would calm down. Lupicinus did not have the nerve to stop them, and so he let them go. As soon as they were outside the city walls, Fritigern and his colleagues saw that the situation was past retrieving. Leaping to their horses amid the enthusiastic shouts of their men, they declared that the Romans had broken their agreement, and that now it was war.

V

THE OUTBREAK OF WAR

The Gothic rebellion fell like a catastrophe on the region around Marcianople. The warriors were filled with rage because of the treatment they had been subjected to, and they had to feed their families. They quickly procured horses and started scouring the countryside for miles around, burning farms, killing farmers, and carrying off their possessions. Lupicinus, as military commander of the province, had to deal with this emergency; he could have referred it to the emperor and requested him to intervene, but Lupicinus decided that he was capable of coping on his own. Clearly, sending Valens a report on the Gothic rebellion that he, Lupicinus, had crushed would have had a much better effect on his career than asking the emperor for reinforcements. Therefore, in great haste, Lupicinus gathered all the troops within his reach and marched out into the open country to give battle. This reaction was an automatic reflex common to all Roman generals, who were so certain of their superiority to the barbarians that they never backed away from any combat with them in the open field.

How many troops Lupicinus may have managed to scrape together is difficult to establish with any certainty. In a large province like Thrace, one of the twelve dioceses into which the empire was divided, there could have been perhaps twenty thousand mobile troops, stationed in towns in the interior, and as many *limitanei*, the frontier guards whose units were dispersed in guard posts all along the course of the Lower Danube. But the *limitanei* could not be withdrawn from their forward positions without endangering the very survival of the empire, and so they need not enter into the calculations. As for the mobile troops, the units specified on paper may not have been actually present; in any case, the regiments were scattered in many towns, some of them hundreds of miles apart. As we know, Lupicinus acted hastily, wishing to eradicate the problem before it grew too large and unpleasant reports began to reach the emperor's ears. In all probability, he gathered only the regiments quartered in Marcianople and the frontier units that had accompanied the barbarian convoy thus far, or rather what remained of those units after the refugees' rebellion. All things considered, he could not have had more than five or six thousand men; but these were professional troops, armed with the heavy gear that was mass-produced in the arms factories of the state.

In those days, the Roman army no longer did battle with the *pilum* and the *gladius*, the stout javelin and the short sword of Caesar's legions; by then, the soldier's principal weapons were the spear, which could be up to two and a half meters (nearly ten feet) long, and the long sword or *spatha*, which was better adapted to close-formation combat in a style similar to that of the ancient Macedonian phalanx. The wooden shield had become round or oval, and the lorica or cuirass had been replaced by an iron coat of mail, which was more practical and easier to produce. Every soldier carried a supply of small javelins—a different model from the *pilum*—and lead-weighted darts, but in practice, combat at a distance was carried on mostly by the archers, of which there were entire regiments, recruited especially in the East. Outwardly, only the design of the steel helmet recalled the legionaries of the old days; but the professionalism and discipline of the regular army was still the same as it had always been.

It is impossible to say how many men Fritigern had at his disposal for the encounter with Lupicinus's force, but the Goths probably outnumbered the Romans. Fritigern was able to field perhaps seven or eight thousand combatants, or maybe even more if he had already been joined by the illegal refugees who had smuggled themselves across the Danube after the Romans weakened their vigilance. Obviously, the total number of refugees was much higher, many tens of thousands of people, but the majority of them were noncombatants: women, old men, the sick, and especially children. The Goths had reached the Roman side of the river without much in the way of good equipment; like all barbarians, they were poor, and most of the warriors had only a lance and a wooden shield. Helmet and sword were luxuries, precious gear reserved for the leaders. A few Goths had armed themselves by despoiling the Romans killed during the clashes outside the wall of Marcianople, but there could not have been many of them.

With everything taken into account, Lupicinus had decent prospects of success. However, he failed, and this was the turning point in this whole history. Because the uprising was in its earliest stages, the Goths must have been, more than anything else, terrified for what they had done; had the army demonstrated an ability to regain control of the situation, perhaps everything would have ended there. But not only did Lupicinus fail to redress the situation; he failed so disastrously that in the end he compromised it definitively, both for the present and for the future. Perhaps the Goths' numerical advantage really was too great, and perhaps desperation gave them a strength that the Romans, even though they were solid professionals, could not match. In any case, when the enemy came into view a few kilometers from Marcianople, Lupicinus arrayed his troops in battle order and waited, certain that he would be able to repulse the barbarian attack. But in fact the attack was delivered with such violence that the Roman lines buckled, began to fall back, and then to break up;

most of the imperial soldiers were slaughtered in the rout. By the time that happened, Lupicinus had already sought safety inside the walls of Marcianople.

Exactly how the battle developed is a subject about which we know very little; the only details to have come down to us are that the Goths attacked with their wooden shields, thrusting them at the enemy, and that in the center of each shield was an iron or bronze boss, from which in many cases protruded a long, sharp point: a real weapon. Through the spaces between the shields, the attackers also struck with lances or—those who had them—with swords. But maybe the truth is simply that there were far more Goths than Lupicinus had anticipated, and in the end the legionaries' lines could not hold. At the end of the day, the Goths went over the battlefield, stripping the fallen of their gear; and if it is true that a great part of the force gathered by Lupicinus fell in the battle, there must have been sufficient helmets, swords, and coats of mail to arm a significant number of Gothic warriors.

We do not know whether Fritigern stopped and pondered the situation. As we shall see later on, he was, from an intellectual point of view, not an ordinary barbarian at all, and he knew how to think in strategic terms; therefore, he likely gave himself over to a great deal of reflection after the first flush of victory passed. Two things seemed evident: One, that after such a slaughter, the Goths had burned their bridges forever, and there was no going back; and two, that they were now masters of Thrace, or at least of that part of it that was open countryside. None of the Roman garrisons bottled up in the big cities was strong enough to come out and challenge the Goths, and until the emperor in Antioch decided what to do, no one would be able to impede their movements or stop them from laying waste the country with fire and sword.

* * *

After the Gothic uprising and the defeat of Lupicinus at Marcianople, the Roman authorities could not have failed to consider what the Gothic mercenary troops would do, the ones who had recently flocked into the empire in great numbers to participate in the war that Valens was preparing to fight against Persia. Would they remain loyal to the government that hired and paid them, or would they respond to the call of their race, rise in revolt, and go to the aid of the refugees? Fortunately for the Romans, most of those troops were already in quarters beyond the mountains of Anatolia, not far from the Mesopotamian frontier, and the news may never even have reached them except in a censored form and very long after the fact. Two Gothic chieftains, however, veterans who had been in Valens's service for years, were stationed with their men in Thrace itself and charged with guarding the army's winter quarters near another of the region's large cities, Adrianople. It lay hundreds of miles away from the frontier areas where the other Goths, the refugees, had crossed the Danube; clearly, however, the mercenaries encamped in the vicinity of Adrianople must sooner or later have been informed about what had happened.

The municipal authorities in Adrianople were not at all pleased at having to maintain those troops on their territory, especially since the Goths had little discipline and were much given to plundering. Nonetheless, when their two leaders learned about the rebellion that was spreading like an oil stain through the Danube region, they did not budge. They were mercenaries, they fought for whoever paid them, and they do not appear to have felt any sort of ethnic solidarity with the Goths who were fighting farther north. But Valens, in Antioch, grew worried. As soon as someone reminded him of those Gothic mercenary units stationed so close to the area of the uprising, the emperor immediately sent their commanders orders to move out and join the other mercenary units in Mesopotamia.

Even after they received these messages, the two mercenary commanders, the tribal chieftains Sueridus and Colias, were not even minimally upset. They presented themselves to the city fathers and requested the money and provisions necessary for the long march, guaranteeing that within two days they would set out with their men. At this point, however, something went wrong. According to Ammianus Marcellinus, it was all the fault of the principal magistrate of the city, who evidently fit into the incompetent category and who moreover had a grudge against the mercenaries for some damage they had caused on his lands. This man may already have suspected the Goths of bad faith and their request for a two-day delay seemed to him proof of their treachery; there have been other cases of this sort of paranoia, and they have usually produced catastrophic consequences. In this particular instance, the city magistrate, instead of providing the mercenaries with what they had requested, raised an alarm among the citizenry and ordered the Goths to move out not within two days but at once.

The ultimatum must have astonished the Goths, who were preparing to leave peacefully, in obedience to the emperor's orders, but they quickly determined that the magistrate was speaking in earnest. In fact, the city had armed its citizens by distributing arms and armor from the imperial stores, and the people were on guard in the streets, grimly waiting for the Goths to leave. No one thought to furnish the mercenaries with what they needed, and after a while the whistles and insults coming from the crowd were replaced by stones, and sometime after that, arrows began flying with the stones. Attacked in this way, by civilians in the middle of the street, the Goths remained stunned for a time, unsure of what to do, but eventually they lost patience, drew their swords, and charged the crowd, provoking general panic. A good many bodies, almost all of them civilians, lay dead on the pavement, and at this point the Goths, seeing that their position was now thoroughly compromised, marched out of the city and decided to join Fritigern's rebels, who had already started south after their victorious clash with Lupicinus and were not far away.

Their arrival was greeted with enthusiasm, and in the excitement of the moment, the warriors decided to march on Adrianople with their entire force and avenge themselves on an ungrateful populace. Fortunately for the inhabitants of the city, however, the Goths had no siege machinery, nor did they know how to build any. After a few days, the Gothic commanders could see that they would be unable to take the city and that their men were losing heart. The road they were on, Fritigern decided, led nowhere; it was ridiculous to persist in besieging the town when the country all around was filled with riches within reach of his hand. And so he delivered a famous speech, in which he explained to his people that it would be better to declare peace with city walls and make war on farmers. The Goths knew that the emperor was far away, and for the moment nothing threatened them; they divided themselves into groups, therefore, and began to scour the countryside. Their women, children, and booty remained in safety with the wagons, and contingents of warriors, some of them now mounted on horseback, set out in all directions in search of plunder.

Smoke rose from burned villas and villages all over the province, and the cities filled up with terrified people fleeing the countryside. However, not everyone was frightened; the Goths were able to find some support among the local inhabitants. These were, in part, their compatriots, because Thrace was filled with Goths. Some of those who lived there were prisoners of war, compelled to work as tenant farmers on the imperial estates; some, naturally, were slaves, the same Gothic slaves who had flooded the markets for many years; and some were youngsters whom their parents had bartered just a few weeks earlier in exchange for something to eat. All of them deserted or fled at the first opportunity and joined their people, and then they served as guides for the warriors, leading them to the richest villages where reserve supplies were stored. But the slaves were not the only ones who joined the rebels; there were also many inhabitants of Thrace who no longer felt loyal to an empire that crushed them with taxes and yet was unable to defend them in time of danger. People arrived at the Goths' encampments daily, offering to accompany them to a store of grain or some rich person's hiding place. The Goths made no difficulties about receiving them, and their contingents grew in numbers and strength with each passing day.

VI

THE BATTLE BY THE WILLOWS

And what was the government doing? The idea of having to abandon his preparations for war against Persia must have pained Valens deeply, but in the end, the fat, one-eyed emperor—who was forty-eight years old and must have known he did not have much time left, since by the standards of those days he was almost an old man—gave in. He sent one of his collaborators to Persia, with orders to try to make peace and salvage whatever was salvageable; and the regiments that had gathered along the Mesopotamian border were sent back, by forced marches, to Thrace, under the command of two of Valens's generals: Trajanus and Profuturus.

The source for this information, Ammianus Marcellinus, was a career military man, and he had a decent understanding of military things. According to him, Trajanus and Profuturus were a couple of peacetime generals, skilled at intriguing in the corridors of the palace, but clueless about how to make war. In a situation like the one that had arisen in Thrace, the Romans needed to apply counterguerrilla methods, because the enemy was weighed down with booty and had been forced to divide into groups in order to be able to live off the land. The Romans needed to organize search parties in force and be content with rounding up one group after another. And they needed to locate the enemy camps and attack them by surprise, even if only with small assault units, to free prisoners and to recover booty; and little by little, the enemy would grow weaker. But Trajanus and Profuturus did not have the perspicacity, and perhaps not even the ability, to organize search parties and wait patiently for their successes. Besides, the nervous emperor might well have told them that he wanted results, and straightaway. In any case, instead of scouring the territory methodically and trying to intercept the Gothic plunderers one group at a time, the Roman army, fresh from Mesopotamia, formed a single column and marched toward the place where the majority of the Goths were encamped. Trajanus and Profuturus were resolved to meet them in a pitched battle, as Lupicinus had already done.

This time, however, the Goths knew that their enemy was stronger than before, and they had no intention of waiting for the Romans to attack. Fritigern called together all his troops, assembled all the wagons in a single, immense train, and then, weighed down by booty and also by thousands of prisoners, began a retreat to the mountainous regions of central Thrace. There, master of the mountain passes, with his people encamped in impregnable positions and his line of retreat secure, Fritigern halted and seemed ready to give battle. The Roman generals led their forces to the foot of the mountains, but then they in their turn had the good sense not to attack. The enemy, after all, had shut himself up in those heights and it would cost him a mighty effort to get out; therefore, there was no reason to run any risks. The Goths awaited the attack for a while; then they continued their retreat northward, exiting the mountains at the farthest point and marching on toward the Danube delta. They appeared to have had enough, to have decided to cross the river again and return to their country, with all the booty, the livestock, and the male and female slaves they had acquired in so many months of undisturbed plundering. The Romans followed them, step for step, though it appeared that neither army really wanted to fight.

* * *

The two armies had almost reached the Danube, the Goths retreating slowly, with their long lines of ox-drawn wagons and tens of thousands of civilians in their train, and the Romans following them at a prudent distance, waiting for a favorable opportunity. The Goths made camp at a place called Ad Salices, "By the Willows." This place has been identified as very close to the Danube delta, in what is today the Dobrogea region of Romania, not far from the Black Sea coast and the ancient town of Tomis, where the poet Ovid died in exile. It was then in one of the farthest corners of the empire; a march of one or two more days would have taken the barbarians to its border, and perhaps they planned to cross the river by going through the delta itself, through its swamps and shallow pools. In the meantime, they set up camp at Ad Salices in their customary way, with all their wagons forming a circle, like the wagon trains of the American West, except that the Goths' circle had a diameter of several hundred yards. Inside this wooden fortress, which Ammianus called a *carrago*, the women lit the fires and prepared the meals; the Goths' horses were also kept inside the ring, as was the great throng of bound prisoners. And the warriors reposed there, too, as befits warriors when no fighting is going on. A few squadrons were sent out in search of forage and provisions.

But not far from there, in the Roman camp, Valens's generals were joined by a general in the service of Gratian, the emperor of the West, who had sent him with a few reinforcements to lend a hand in the emergency. The reinforcements were little more than symbolic because the commanding generals in Gaul had refused to transfer any of the troops serving along the Rhine frontier, and because many new, local recruits, faced with the prospect of having to go to war in the East, had simply deserted. The new arrival was the commander of Emperor Gratian's household guard, Richomer, who was also of barbarian origin—Frankish, to be precise. There was nothing strange about this; the Roman army had always taken in immigrants without distinctions of race, and by this time so many generals fell into this category, second- or even third-generation immigrants, that in reality nothing barbarian remained about them but their names, and perhaps their blond hair. In the most racist circles, from time to time, such men were accused of being untrustworthy, but the truth is that almost all of them were Romanized or Hellenized, and they were often even better educated than their colleagues: more than one of the Franks, Sarmatians, and even Goths who made their careers in the imperial army can be found among the correspondents of the great Greek rhetoricians or the fathers of the church.

The three Roman generals, then, held a council about how to proceed. With their joined forces, they felt they were stronger than the barbarians, even though Ammianus Marcellinus maintained that the Romans were inferior to them in purely numerical terms; in any case, they decided to take the initiative. It was agreed that as soon as the Goths, bored or unnerved by the stay, broke camp and resumed their march, the Romans would attack the rear guard of their convoy, which was where the majority of the prisoners and the booty-laden wagons could always be found, lagging behind. In the worst outcome, the Roman generals reasoned, the enemy would avoid combat by accelerating the pace of the march, and even then the Romans would be able to recover a good deal of booty. If, on the other hand, the Goths accepted battle, they would do so in the most unfavorable conditions, and then perhaps the imperial forces would get the opportunity to resolve the campaign in one fell swoop and put a successful end to the war.

* * *

Inside their wagon-circle in that place with the innocent name, By the Willows, the Goths knew the Romans were nearby, and they also knew the imperial generals planned to attack them as soon as they got under way, at the moment when their column was most vulnerable. Ammianus Marcellinus, our only source for this episode, made clear that the Goths knew everything: Deserters, he said, gave them the information. Ammianus did not even comment upon this fact, so obvious did it seem to him. We think of Romans and Goths as two discrete opposing forces, but they were, in fact, more complex. The imperial army was filled with barbarian volunteers, loyal to the emperor and ready to die fighting against their countrymen for the glory of Rome; but it also contained conscripts enlisted by force, who were waiting only for the right moment to desert. On the other side, the Goths' camp was crowded with prisoners anxiously hoping to be liberated by the soldiers, while others, fugitive slaves or deserters, wanted nothing to do with the government and had decided to link their fate to that of the barbarian rebels.

Deserters, then, informed the Gothic princes of the Romans' intentions, whereupon the Goths, at first, opted for the simplest solution: They did not move at all. Soon, however, they realized their situation could not be prolonged indefinitely. Seeing no other way out of their position, they decided they would have to accept battle. The princes sent dispatch riders to call back all the units that were out foraging; one by one, they returned to camp. With every squadron that returned, the Goths felt stronger, a little more inclined to run the risk of a fight. By the time everyone was back inside the wagon-ring, however, evening had descended, and although the excitement in the barbarian camp was at a fever pitch, it was too late to go out and do battle. As Ammianus described, "The entire multitude of barbarians, still crowded within the circle of their wagons and beside themselves with savage rage, clamored to confront the worst danger at once, undiscouraged by their leaders." In all probability, sanitary conditions in the camp, the scarcity of fresh food, and the tension caused by the sort of siege they were under combined to make everyone wish only to burst out of the circle and face the danger. But the Goths had to wait for the following day. They sat down to eat, but no one slept.

The Roman camp was but a short distance away, and the imperial troops, who could hear the Goths roaring, were also well aware that something big was about to happen, and did not sleep either. The soldiers told themselves that their cause was just, and that God, or the gods, would come to their aid; but at the same time, they knew that their enemies were a great multitude and that they were savages, worse than wild beasts. For this reason, the veterans in the Roman camp shook their heads, anxious about the outcome of the impending fight.

* * *

The next morning, everyone made ready for battle. In the Roman camp, trumpets called every soldier to join his unit and take up his designated position. The barbarians, too, sounded their trumpets, and at the sound the Gothic warriors fell into formations as though they had been trained. According to their custom, the barbarians renewed the oath to their commanders that they had made upon first entering into their retinue, swearing to die rather than abandon them in danger, and brothers in arms made the same pledge to one another. Then the multitude of warriors stepped out of the wagon-circle, not tumultuously but in good order, an ever-increasing mass that spread out over the plain. The Romans were lining up a few hundred yards away, and the last soldiers were hastening to their posts when the commanders saw that the enemy had come out and was about to attack. Then, one by one, the two masses started moving closer to each other, because both of them wished to show that they were unafraid and that they would not refuse combat.

It was one thing, however, to move closer, and another to come into actual contact. We are conditioned by movies to imagine two masses of warriors, each composed of many thousands of men clad in iron armor, rushing upon each other, dealing blows as they come on; but, in fact, that is not the way this battle unfolded. The two armies moved uneasily forward in turn, coming to a halt before colliding; it was not at all clear which of them would have the courage to attack first.

War in ancient times was made up of this and many other rituals. To stoke their own valor and demoralize the enemy, the Romans, in unison, would shout their war cry, for which they used a barbarian word, *barritus*. This word originally referred to the trumpeting of an elephant, and the Romans' cry was indeed more animal than human, a kind of mooing that began on a low note and gradually rose to a deafening howl. The Roman soldiers—some of whom were immigrants born in foreign lands—had learned this battle-roar from none other than Germanic tribesmen.

The Goths, for their part, defied their enemies in accordance with ancestral custom: They advanced into no-man's-land, presented themselves, spoke in praise of their own forefathers, and promised not to dishonor them that day. Two hundred years after these events, the last Gothic king in Italy, Totila, would adhere to the same ritual before the battle of Taginae (modern-day Gualdo Tadino), putting his horse through some acrobatic paces and demonstrating his skill at handling the lance, as if his ancestors were there watching him. Soldiers on both sides screwed up their courage by insulting the enemy; many of those who were close enough started flinging their javelins, and the archers, well hidden behind the last ranks, shot their arrows. These missile weapons didn't cause much damage, but with a little luck they could make the enemy nervous, and javelins and arrows often stuck in shields, eventually weakening and weighing them down so much they became unusable. In this gradual way, the battle was joined. Here and there, some overexcited groups lost patience, moved forward, and challenged the enemy to combat, "and amid all this shouting in different languages," Ammianus said, "skirmishing efforts began."

* * *

How long the two armies remained a javelin's throw apart, turbulently swaying forward and backward, screaming threats and boasts, is not recorded. At length, however, their inhibitory restraints fell away, and without anyone having given the order, the two walls of shields moved forward and collided with each other.

Several thousand men were on each side, the majority of them infantry, and all of them armed in more or less the same way, because the Goths had had quite enough time to procure themselves Roman helmets and coats of mail. The cavalry milled nervously around the two masses of warriors, ready to pursue and cut down those who ran away, but without much possibility of really influencing the outcome of the battle, given the density of the pike formations; the archers and slingers remained at a distance, watching for a chance to do some damage by bringing down a warrior careless about covering himself with his shield. But in the end the battle came down to two great throngs of soldiers, demented by stress and fear, all crowded on top of one another, trying to take shelter behind not only their own shields but also their neighbor's, with the conditioned reflex that the ancient authors claim was typical of all combatants. Once the two masses made contact, the only way to survive was to push forward, either by trying to stab your adversary from below or by throwing him down and crushing him under your shield. Should anyone lose his head, cast aside his weapons, and try to flee, he was lost: The cavalry would chase him down and kill him. The only thing to do was to stay inside the phalanx and keep pushing forward, paying no heed to the dust, the screams, and whomever you were trampling underfoot.

Eventually, it seems, the Roman left wing gave way; in that part of the battlefield, the barbarian shield wall advanced. But the Roman generals had foreseen this development. In ancient armies, the left wing was always the one that held back, precisely because infantry troops carried their shields on their left arms, and every man, as he advanced, tried to hide behind his neighbor's shield and therefore tended to move forward to the right; and it was for this very reason that Richomer, who as the highest-ranking officer was in command that day, had amassed reserve troops on his left, and these halted the barbarian advance.

When darkness fell, the battle was still going on, even though by then no one could have been much inclined to keep fighting. Ancient battles were arduous, the majority of soldiers fought without interruption from the first moment, and no matter how rigorously they had been trained, they could not last more than a few hours. A little at a time, as it happened, some units lost contact; those that had been compelled to retreat came to a halt and stayed where they were instead of returning to the attack; in the end, the two armies found themselves separated again. Slowly, the Goths withdrew to safety inside their wagon-circle; the Romans in turn retired to their camp. According to their custom, they tried to carry back with them the bodies of the officers who had been killed, so that they could be buried with the proper rites; the other dead were left behind to be devoured by carrion birds, and years later, Ammianus observed, whoever passed that way could see the battlefield, still white with their bleaching bones.

* * *

We cannot state a figure for the losses on that day, but they were surely heavy on both sides, if not enormous; in ancient battles the real massacre began when one of the two armies was put to flight and pursuers could slaughter fugitives without risk to themselves. As long as a battle unfolded without winners or losers, as happened at the Willows, casualties were probably more limited; nevertheless, what with the dead, the wounded, the injured, and those in shock, the combat readiness of both armies must have been drastically diminished.

The Romans had learned the bitterest lesson. Their enemy was at least as numerous as they, if not more so, and was not afraid to fight, not intimidated at the idea of facing the imperial legions. If he had fought today, they reasoned, he would be able to fight again tomorrow, while the emperor's generals, by contrast, were not sure they could do the same. In a regular army, casualties have more weight; the loss of officers or noncommissioned officers demoralizes the troops, and the loss of a half or a third of its men can suffice to destroy the cohesion of an entire regiment. The Romans were nearly at the farthest limits of their empire. They had met the enemy, hoping to finish him, and they had failed. To remain where they were and try again the following day was to court disaster. Above all, some of the regiments that had fought at the Willows, along with Richomer, their commander, belonged to the emperor of the West; they had come to help his uncle, Valens, smother a barbarian rebellion, but getting themselves killed to the last man in order to defend that extreme margin of the eastern empire was not part of their mission. The night after the battle, the Roman generals drew their conclusions, and the next day what remained of their army started marching south.

The Roman columns retreated for several days, marching more than sixty miles and stopping only when they reached Marcianople. As for the Goths, their casualties had been so heavy that they remained shut up inside their wagon-circle for a week, burying their dead and celebrating the funeral rites of their people. Among the fallen chieftains, those who were pagans were probably buried together with their horses and perhaps also their favorite female slaves, who were strangled on the spot so that they might accompany their master into the next life. For the Christians, an Arian priest probably recited the funeral service, perhaps even in Greek, while the ritual lamentations of the women and the singing of songs praising the valor of the heroic dead accompanied those in both categories. Then, once the rituals and the purifications were completed, the warriors began to leave the wagon-circle to reconnoiter their surroundings; they returned with the news that the Roman soldiers were indeed gone.

For a period of time, the Goths continued to live off the resources of the plains along the Danube delta, robbing peasants, carrying off supplies from farms, slaughtering livestock. At length, however, they realized that finding enough to eat in that underdeveloped region was becoming more and more difficult. Then, seeing that the Romans had not dared to attack them again after the battle—that they had, in fact, vanished—the Gothic princes decided against resuming their northward march, crossing the Danube, and reentering their country; they chose instead to head south, into the agriculturally rich Thracian hinterland, in search of new provinces to plunder.

VII

THE WAR GOES ON

After the battle by the Willows, the Roman generals no longer had the courage to confront the Goths in the open field. It may seem strange that an empire that maintained an army of five or six hundred thousand men couldn't manage to gather enough troops to crush an army of rebels that could not have numbered more than ten or twelve thousand, but in fact the empire's very immensity rendered its power ineffective. Most of its soldiers were *limitanei*, border guards, and they were scattered in innumerable garrisons along thousands of miles of frontier, from Hadrian's Wall in Scotland to the oases of the Arabian Desert. The mobile forces, which stood ready to intervene wherever there was an emergency, were nonetheless dispersed in hundreds of military depots inside the empire. All the provinces needed troops, not only to prevent barbarian raids but also to combat brigands, discourage rebellions, maintain public order, and collect taxes. Count Lupicinus's defeat at Marcianople had demonstrated that the mobile forces stationed in Thrace were insufficient to put an end to the rebellion. While the battle by the Willows was not decisive, part of the troops that Valens had prepared to invade Persia had been badly mauled, as had the first reinforcements to arrive from the West. The Roman army always operated within narrow margins, and for the moment it had no more leeway; it could not risk another battle.

But the Romans could exploit the terrain, and this the generals began to do at once. With their northward march, which had brought them almost to the Danube, the Goths had left the most fertile parts of the province, and now they were camped in the steppe-land south of the river, in a region that the Romans had attempted to populate long before with settlers and deportees. However, the land didn't have enough resources to support such a great multitude as the Goths, including tens of thousands of civilians in addition to their fighting forces, and perhaps an equal number of oxen and horses, all requiring maintenance. The Roman generals evacuated the region, ordering that all the reserves of provisions and the majority of the people should be collected and brought to the fortified cities, which the Goths could not besiege; in practice, these measures left the barbarians masters of a countryside that was sterile and without resources. Sooner or later the Goths, if they wished to avoid starvation, would have to return to the south, but to do that, they would have to cross once again what the Romans called the Haemus Mountains, the eastern extension of the Balkan range. These were wild heights, crossed by few roads, where the Romans would need only to close off a few mountain passes in order to block the progress of that great multitude of people, beasts, and wagons. Therefore, the imperial troops set to work, constructing barriers across every pass. Roman military training had always placed great emphasis on developing a capacity for fast, hard, organized work when necessity required it, transforming soldiers into woodcutters, carpenters, and masons, and now that capacity was put to good use. When the Goths moved south and started to cross the mountains, they found all the passes blocked, with palisades, earthworks, and even stone walls, and behind them the Romans were waiting.

* * *

A year had already passed since the Goths massed on the north bank of the Danube, begging to be received into the empire. The battle by the Willows, along with the Roman retreat southward and the sealing of the Balkan passes, took place in the summer of 377; at least, that is the way we moderns count the years. The Romans didn't count them; they designated them with the names of the two consuls for each year, so the events just mentioned were referred to as having taken place "under the consulship of Gratian and Merobaudes."

The names of the two consuls for that year elicit various reflections on the nature of the empire. One of the two, Gratian, was the reigning emperor of the West, because it was normal practice for one consulship to be held by the emperor; that year, Gratian was consul for the fourth time. But the other consul, Flavius Merobaudes, was one of those soldiers of Germanic origin, an immigrant or the son of immigrants—as is clear from his name—who had not only made a career in the army but was also perfectly integrated into the ruling class of the empire, so much so that he could rise to the consulship. Even though the office no longer entailed any political power, the consulship was almost sacred to the Romans and enjoyed a level of prestige difficult for us to imagine today; the fact that such a height could be reached even by foreign politicians and soldiers suggests how open and composite the empire's governing class was.

Everyone knew that winters in those latitudes could be extremely harsh, and as the summer waned the Roman generals started thinking that cold and hunger would do the job of eliminating the Goths if they remained blockaded in the mountains. Valens, still in Antioch and not at all satisfied with the news reaching him from the front, had sent one of his most trusted generals, Saturninus, to Thrace with all available reinforcements, so the troops manning the barriers in the Balkan passes were under a new commander. Saturninus arrived in the Roman encampment at the very moment when the Goths were beginning to realize they were in a trap. For several days, furiously and in the end desperately, the barbarians attacked the palisades and earthworks that barred their way, but they never succeeded in forcing a passage, and Saturninus grew convinced that he had them in the palm of his hand.

Though the passages through which they could descend from the mountains and spread out over the rich plains to the south were indeed blocked, communications to the north, to the Danube plain and the steppe, were open, and so the Goths sent for help. They turned to other tribes of pastoralists and mounted warriors, first the Alans and then even a few clans of Huns. Not long before, terror of the Huns had driven the Goths from their land, but now the situation was changed. The Goths had established a bridgehead in Roman territory; even Hunnish leaders, primitive though they were, could understand that the prospects of conquest and plunder were too handsome to ignore. Autumn had barely begun, winter was still far off, and the news that started to arrive at Saturninus's command post grew more and more worrisome: It was said that large bands of Alans and Huns were crossing the Danube and heading south.

* * *

At this point, Saturninus made a fatal decision, although it may well have been the only choice he had left. It was one thing to barricade the mountain passes and stop the advance of the Gothic train, which with all the wagons and livestock must have been well over ten miles long, moved slowly, weighed down by booty and slaves, and once its location was determined, could easily be blocked by closing only a few roads. But it was another thing altogether to block the passage of extremely mobile cavalry troops, men accustomed to undertaking swift, sudden raids and capable of using any road or path, of discovering unknown shortcuts, and perhaps even of appearing behind the Roman camp, attacking it by surprise, and cutting the Romans' lines of retreat.

This was a terrifying prospect, and Saturninus decided he could not run that risk; better, he thought, to gather all his troops, descend from the mountains—winter was coming on for the Romans, too—lead the army to safety in the fortified cities of the plain, and reconsider his strategy, with a view to solving the problem the following year. The result, however, was that as soon as the Goths realized that the enemy had abandoned the fortifications and the passes were open, they crossed the mountains; then they, too, spilled out onto the Thracian plain.

Again, just as in the previous year, the violence and the looting began. Thrace was large, and the Goths, together with the bands of Huns and Alans who had come to join them, scoured the land with impunity. In order to spend the winter in quarters, the Roman troops had been obliged to disperse to various cities, where the supplies of barley, wine, and lard indispensable for their sustenance were stored. The Goths were out in the open, camped in their wagons and exposed to the winter, but the countryside was undefended, and everything they could find in it was theirs for the taking. Once again, Ammianus Marcellinus's history recounted the sad story of burned and plundered farms, of women brutalized and violated, of boys and girls carried off as slaves. In order to escape the barbarians' atrocities, the local inhabitants fled the region en masse, in such numbers that a generation later there were still large depopulated areas in Thrace, impossible to travel through because they lacked human inhabitants. Some of the Thracian refugees got as far as Italy, where they found work as laborers on the great estates of the Po plain or in some cases sold themselves into slavery as a means of avoiding starvation.

As if all this weren't enough, the entry of the Roman troops into winter quarters was badly handled by Saturninus, another person who may with some justice be suspected of incompetence, a characteristic that turned up a bit too frequently among the high officials and bureaucrats of the eastern empire. Some units made for Dibaltum, a town on the shore of the Black Sea, a good place to pass the winter; but they were still encamped outside the city walls when the barbarians fell on them in a surprise attack. These were select units, some of the best infantry regiments in the empire, including one of the most famous, called the Cornuti because the troops wore horns on their helmets. This regiment's fame went back to the time of Constantine, and it had so distinguished itself at the battle of the Mulvian Bridge (AD 312) that a relief depicting one of its soldiers, horns and all, can still be seen today on the Arch of Constantine in Rome. With them there was at least one regiment of Scutarii, the heavy cavalry of the imperial guard; in fact, the commanding officer of the entire imperial force at Dibaltum was the commander of this same regiment, the tribune Barzimeres, probably, judging from his name, an Armenian or a Persian. No one had warned Barzimeres that the enemy was so close, and the tribune barely had time to marshal his troops. He managed to hold out for a long time, but his men were heavily outnumbered, and in the end the barbarians overwhelmed them.

* * *

It was, perhaps, no accident that the Goths surprised Barzimeres's force in the open and destroyed it. The Gothic leaders were by no means as uncouth as the Romans believed them to be; they were princes, long accustomed to negotiating with the Romans, they probably spoke Latin and Greek, more than one of them was Christian, and they had a pretty clear idea of what they wanted and of the strategies they should follow. They knew that they and their people faced enticing possibilities that could also become mortally dangerous, and they proceeded cautiously, careful not to make a false move but always on the alert to seize every available opportunity. They were perfectly aware that the Romans, having abandoned the Balkan passes, had retreated to the plain in some disorder, and that they had no more intention of giving battle. The Gothic princes further knew that the Roman system provided for the serving troops' survival during the winter months by distributing the men, in small groups, to several different cities and towns; and having perceived that the Roman generals they faced were not original thinkers, the Goths could be certain they would stick to standard procedure.

The Gothic leaders, therefore, decided that in the remaining days of fall, before winter made it impossible to move quickly from place to place with a great number of horses, they would not be satisfied merely with plundering the country and amassing quantities of booty; they would also seek to surprise isolated Roman contingents and destroy them separately. Having come down from the Balkan gorges starving and at the end of their strength, the warriors had profited from plundering and were now well nourished, Ammianus observed, "with more refined food than usual," namely what they found in the kitchens and cellars of rich country villas. Moreover, having been joined by the Huns and the Alans, they had a great many horses, and after all the fighting they had done, every warrior surely had a coat of mail, a helmet, and a sword, all taken from a fallen Roman soldier. The barbarians were winning the war, and they had every intention of pressing their advantage.

A spy or a deserter notified the Gothic leaders that some regiments from the western empire, those sent by Gratian to assist his uncle, were camped near the city of Beroea, at the foot of the Balkan mountain range. These troops, survivors of the battle by the Willows, had by this time been in Thrace for many months, and their commander, Frigeridus, was a much talked-about man. Judging from his name, he too was a son of Germanic immigrants, and some people suspected him of being secretly in sympathy with the Goths. Having suffered an opportune attack of gout before the commencement of hostilities at the Willows, Frigeridus had been unable to participate in that battle. As one may imagine, this gout attack was also the subject of a great deal of gossip. Frigeridus's detachment, isolated, combat-damaged, and led by a questionable general, seemed the ideal victim, and the council of Gothic princes decided to send the bulk of their troops to Beroea, there to attack and destroy the Roman force as they had destroyed Barzimeres and his command.

* * *

Although Frigeridus was a man people gossiped about, he also knew his business. Ammianus Marcellinus, who was not one to spare colleagues criticism when he thought they had not done a good job, called Frigeridus a careful, diligent leader who never wasted the lives of his soldiers. From his encampment at the bottom of the Balkan slopes, he sent out scouts far and wide and quickly learned that the bulk of the Gothic forces had moved out in his direction, intent on attacking him. Frigeridus evaluated the situation and decided it made no sense to stay where he was and wait for the attack. Behind and above him lay the mountain gorges that led to the western side of the Balkans and the region that the Romans called Illyricum, which for us, broadly speaking, is the former Yugoslavia. This territory was part of the western empire, and Frigeridus's first duty was to defend it and to prevent the barbarians from bursting into the western provinces as well. Therefore, he decided to break camp and withdraw through the valley of the Maritsa River, which the Romans called the Hebrus, to the Succi Pass, through which it was possible to descend into Macedonia.

The Gothic forces followed him closely, together with other barbarian groups that had recently crossed the Danube, taking advantage of the collapse of the frontier defenses, the withdrawal of the Roman garrisons, and the panic that had spread throughout the province. Some of these groups were Taifali, a people who spoke a Gothic language; Ammianus Marcellinus told a curious story about them that offers a little deeper insight into the barbarian universe. "We have heard," Ammianus said, "that these Taifali are a debased people, so immersed in a life of shameful obscenity that among them boys are paired with men and lie with them in a compact of unspeakable lust, consuming the flower of their age in these polluted practices. But thereafter, if a youngster grown to manhood catches a wild boar or slays a huge bear by himself, he is cleansed from the filth of this defilement." Looking past Ammianus's righteous indignation and considering this account from an anthropological standpoint, one can recognize the rites of a warrior tribe, where the initiation of the young includes a period of sexual union with older men, and where a test of courage or physical strength marks the passage to adulthood. The Romans were ill equipped to appreciate this sort of thing, and we can see how easily the stereotype of corrupt and immoral barbarians could take root in their way of thinking. But these tribes of nomadic steppe warriors were hard cases, and while their raiding parties were running free in the Balkans, the empire of the East was sinking into a crisis which no one knew how to escape.

* * *

Withdrawing to Illyricum through the Balkan Mountains, Frigeridus and his army were in a dangerous situation, the kind where a mistake would carry a heavy price. Several groups of Goths and Taifali, for the most part on horseback, followed the Romans. The barbarians were sure of themselves, and while they continued their pursuit, predatory bands also spread out to plunder the country. Had the barbarian cavalry surprised Frigeridus's column while it was negotiating a difficult passage, the Romans would probably have been cut to pieces. But while he withdrew slowly toward the Succi Pass, his scouts kept him informed of the barbarians' movements, and after learning that many of the bands following him had come together and were advancing along a single road, Frigeridus prepared an ambush. When the pursuing barbarians found themselves facing the Roman infantry drawn up in battle array, they attacked at once, certain that they had come upon his rear guard; but the Romans appeared on their flanks and surrounded them. A massacre began, in which there was no small element of revenge, and Frigeridus "might have slaughtered the lot of them to the last man, so that not even a messenger would have survived to report the disaster." However, after the barbarian chiefs fell, the survivors threw themselves on their knees and begged for mercy.

Even though the Roman Empire was by this time officially Christian, the Romans did not consider themselves in any way bound to show charity to their enemies and had no problem massacring prisoners and even civilians. But over a long period of time, the imperial administration had grown accustomed to considering manpower, even barbarian manpower, as a precious resource to be husbanded as far as possible, and apparently this notion had been hammered into military heads as well. And so Frigeridus stopped the massacre and accepted the barbarians' surrender. We don't know how many there were, but at least a few hundred and perhaps even more, most of them Taifali and all of them sturdy adult males. Frigeridus had them put into chains and brought them along with him in his retreat through the mountains. When the army reached the other side of the range, Frigeridus turned his prisoners over to the officials in charge of immigrant allocation, who were delighted to get their hands on so many workers. The western empire, too, contained vast unpopulated regions with not enough laborers to work the land, including parts of Gaul, mostly because of barbarian raids, as well as in Italy, especially in the Po plain. The Goths and Taifali captured by Frigeridus were in fact sent to Italy and settled as tenant farmers on state properties in the Po lowlands around Modena, Reggio, and Parma. That the government did not hesitate, in the midst of a crisis so profound as the one that was laying waste the Balkans, to take hundreds of barbarian prisoners—members of extremely warlike tribes—and transfer them to workplaces in Italy itself, is an indication of the need for manpower that gripped the empire and also a sign of the belief in their own superiority and security that the Romans, in spite of everything, continued to maintain in respect to the barbarians.

VIII

VALENS MOVES

The year 378 opened with decidedly troubling prospects for the empire. The barbarians were masters of the rich Thracian countryside, which stretched from the Danube to the outskirts of Constantinople. All the Roman army units present in the region, including the reinforcements sent from the western empire, had been compelled to shut themselves up inside fortified cities or had withdrawn toward Illyricum as Frigeridus and his army had done. From the walls of the capital, people could see barbarian bands roaming the countryside, and they began to fear that sooner or later, the enemy was going to approach; camp in front of the city gates, and lay siege to the metropolis. Everyone in the Roman world knew about this threat that was consuming the empire's strength, and there was but one question in the public's mind: What were the emperors going to do?

Valens, who was about to complete his fiftieth year, was still in Antioch, and given that all the generals sent to put down the rebellion had been defeated one after another, his was the most difficult decision. His nephew Gratian, emperor of the West, was a much younger man, and some thought it incumbent upon him to take the situation in hand by intervening in person with the bulk of the western army—which was traditionally more expert and more imbued with fighting spirit than the army of the East. Rumors spread through the cities of the empire, were repeated in the markets and barracks and along the frontiers, and eventually reached even the ears of the barbarians across the borders. A soldier who served in the imperial guard, a member of the Alamanni tribe, was called home on urgent business, obtained leave, and returned to his tribal lands on the far side of the Rhine. While he was home, he reported that all the peoples who bordered on the eastern provinces had sworn an oath to destroy the Roman Empire, and that Gratian was about to depart with his entire army to go to the aid of his uncle Valens. We don't know whether the soldier related these things in good faith, to amaze his neighbors with his secret knowledge, or whether he was doing an adroit bit of spying. It may be that he was indeed in good faith, because he went back to the imperial army as if nothing were the matter and resumed his service in the barracks; but the emperor had him punished anyway, for talking too much.

The Alamanni listened to this news, and several groups of their young men, upon learning that the empire's soldiers were being transferred to the East, came to the conclusion that this was a good opportunity for cross-border raids into Roman territory. Thus Gratian, who had gathered his troops and was preparing to set out for the Balkans, was forced to change his plans and undertake a punitive expedition across the Rhine. These large-scale police operations usually ended in the same way, with a triumphant display of burned villages and massacred civilians, and with barbarian leaders hastily begging to make peace. This time, however, the Alamanni, informed that Gratian was about to attack them, did something they had never done before: They successfully reached an agreement with all their tribes and assembled in one place an unprecedented number of warriors. Gratian's punitive expedition across the Rhine turned into a full-scale campaign, and even though in the end the Alamanni were defeated and compelled to ask for peace, many months passed. The spring of the year 378 was already over, and the army of the West had not yet set out across the Balkan Mountains to go to Valens's aid.

* * *

Valens, meanwhile, bestirred himself. He could not remain in Antioch while the barbarians were pillaging and plundering the very suburbs of his capital, so he decided to depart, though no doubt reluctantly. The emperor and his retinue, the enormous train of the imperial court, with secretaries and eunuchs, priests and guards, concubines and slaves, crossed the dusty Anatolian plains and reached Constantinople at last, after a journey that must have lasted more than a month. The emperor's sojourn in the city, however, was exceedingly brief; despite the public works he had financed and the great aqueduct he was having built, Valens was unpopular among the citizens of the capital, and he did not like them much, either. Shortly after Valens's brother, Valentinian, appointed him emperor of the East, the people of Constantinople had thrown their support to General Procopius, commander of the garrison in the capital, who attempted to usurp the imperial throne; Valens, therefore, had no love for the metropolis on the Bosporus and stayed there as little as possible.

As soon as he arrived, he became aware of the heavy atmosphere hanging over the city: The people were frightened by the news of the atrocities committed by the Goths and resentful of a government that could not seem to bring the matter to a successful conclusion. At the games in the Hippodrome, Valens was hooted and whistled at, and before long, his subjects passed from cries of protest and whistling to incidents in the public squares. Deciding he had had enough, the emperor left the capital and went to the imperial villa of Melanthias, a luxurious country residence about twelve miles from Constantinople.

There, finally free to work, he set about gathering all available troops, intending to liquidate the Gothic problem once and for all. As the units arrived from their various garrisons, the men were fed a special mess to replenish their strength, they received their back pay, and then they lined up on the parade ground to hear the emperor's speeches, in which he exhorted them to show themselves worthy of their fame. Morale was high, or so it seems, perhaps more because of the special food and the back pay than because of Valens's speeches. In the course of a few weeks, the emperor brought together all the mobile regiments that were still stationed in the eastern provinces and also the entire cavalry detachment of the imperial guard, which had accompanied him from Antioch. When he was satisfied that he had accumulated a sufficient force, Valens decided to move.

By this time high summer had arrived, and the Goths with their wagon trains, more and more heavily laden with spoils and prisoners, continued to rove about Thrace undisturbed. The defeat inflicted on them by Frigeridus had weakened them, but in the fine, warm weather, they were continually being joined by new groups, fresh from crossing the Danube and eager to share in their countrymen's great good fortune. If something was not done to stop them, the barbarians would keep getting stronger and stronger, and the public mood throughout the empire grew increasingly somber. Clearly, the emperor could afford to wait no longer. His nephew Gratian had finished his match with the Alamanni, and there was precise information that he was on his way to Thrace with the bulk of the army of the West. The couriers reported that Gratian was in ill health, and that bands of enemy cavalry were steadily attacking his vanguard to impede his march, but there was no doubt that sooner or later, he would reach Thrace. Together, the two emperors planned to close the barbarians in a pincer movement and annihilate them.

* * *

While Valens's army was readying itself to march toward the Thracian interior and its infestation of Gothic marauders, the emperor and his generals discussed plans for the campaign. In a conflict that by this time had been going on for two years, experience had taught them they must never give battle except when the circumstances were absolutely favorable and they were certain of success. One of our sources, the Greek writer Eunapius, described the situation according to a scheme typical of the ancient sensibility, a scheme that reduced everything to a question of culture: If one had been well educated and had read the proper books, he would have learned from the experience of the ancients that he must never directly confront an enemy pushed to desperation, with no way out and therefore ready to fight to the death. To destroy such an enemy, the most economical method was to draw things out and try to cut his supply lines. If this succeeded, the enemy's very numbers would become a disadvantage to him, because the more there were, the harder it would be for them to stave off starvation.

Eunapius seems to imply that Valens failed to grasp these things because he had not studied enough, and had not gone to the right schools. But actually Valens, at least in the beginning, seems to have understood very well that this was not a time for the army to put its head down and march forward against the enemy. Even though he had not read it in books, the experience of those two years of war had taught him that one could win a lot by risking a little—namely by organizing what today we would call a counterguerrilla strategy and what the Romans, little given to theoretical reflection and lacking an adequate vocabulary, called by no name at all. Scouring the countryside in small, mobile groups preceded by a large number of scouts, they located the enemy and carried out surprise raids to trap any band incautious enough to step into the net. Organizing operations of this kind required a specialist, and Valens happened to have just such a man at his disposal; his name was Sebastianus.

Our sources all agree that Sebastianus was the best general of his time. He had risen to the top quickly, because the empire had a great need for capable soldiers, and the best ones usually attracted notice. Sebastianus had no vices and lived for war. He was solicitous of his soldiers' welfare, Eunapius said, but he did not pamper them and maintained strict discipline. And therefore, as happens in such cases, he was admired but not beloved. He did not understand corruption, and never sought to enrich himself, and this trait, too, bothered many people. He was loathed by the eunuchs who controlled the entire life of the imperial court and kept an eye on how promotions were granted. Since he was poor, it was all too easy to get rid of him: At the first occasion, they relieved him of his command and pensioned him off. But when the Gothic rebellion broke out, Sebastianus, who was living in retirement in Italy, asked to be returned to service, and for once Valens shut his ears to the eunuchs and recalled him.

Sebastianus, then, was ordered to organize a mobile force and start harassing operations against the Goths with the aim of gradually weakening them while the two imperial armies of Valens and Gratian were still concentrating. When asked how many men he needed, Sebastianus replied that two thousand would suffice, provided he could choose them himself. Valens was pleasantly surprised; until then, all the generals he had dealt with had complained about having too few troops and asked him for reinforcements. Sebastianus explained that if things went as he believed they would, soon other units would be volunteering and competing to serve under him, because he was not, in fact, indifferent to riches; whoever fought well and obeyed orders could get rich fighting under his command, but with spoils taken from the enemy, not with money and goods extorted from civilians, as happened in other units.

This response helps us understand why Sebastianus was so little loved by his colleagues. However, our sources also reveal that he was not merely boasting and that he knew how to take serious action. All available information reported that the barbarians had created two large, permanent encampments: one in the far north, near the Danube, and one at Beroea, on the other or southern side of the Balkan mountain range, in the same spot where Frigeridus and his army had been encamped the previous year. This position dominated the roads leading north as well as those that led west to the western empire; it was as if the barbarians were organizing themselves to transform the pillage of Thrace from an improvised activity into a permanent industry. The two stable camps were linked to each other like fortified, impregnable staging posts, facilitating the movement of spoils and slaves northward, to the land of the Goths. From these fortified camps, predatory bands of raiders regularly sallied forth to scour the countryside, section by section, and then to return laden with booty. One such group of raiders pushed quite far south, to the region around the city of Adrianople; there, however, their captives reported that the emperor was approaching at the head of a powerful army, whereupon the Goths turned back, heading for the safety of their camps.

Sebastianus assembled his two thousand men by selecting a few hundred from each of the best regiments, and with this "task force," as we would call it today, he set off by forced marches in pursuit of the Goths. The Goths had a few days' head start, but their column was slow, laden as they were with plunder, so that the imperial troops had every probability of catching up with them and destroying them. But when Sebastianus and his men, hot on the barbarians' trail, reached the walls of Adrianople, an event occurred that highlighted the climate of panic and collective hysteria that had settled over that part of the empire since the beginning of the Gothic invasion. Fearing some heinous treachery, the citizens of Adrianople refused to open the city gates to the soldiers, and only after long negotiations would they agree to let Sebastianus enter the city alone; the soldiers had to stay outside and bivouac under the walls.

As related earlier, in the early days of the insurrection these citizens had attacked a contingent of Gothic mercenaries, imperial soldiers who had been quartered in the city for some time with the result that the mercenaries, instead of departing for service in Mesopotamia, joined the Gothic rebellion.

These two episodes reveal the extent of the social collapse caused by two years of a war that was in some ways almost a civil conflict. The Goths were not invaders in a traditional sense but rather immigrants and refugees who had rebelled because of the shameful treatment they had received, and who had since welcomed into their ranks a multitude of deserters, escaped criminals, and runaway slaves. By contrast, the soldiers of the imperial army, a great many of whom had been recruited among barbarians and immigrants as well, regularly came to public notice for the arrogance and brutality of their dealings with civilians. Between one and the other, the population of a great city of the empire was practically at a loss to choose, and the citizens ended up heartily detesting both.

At dawn Sebastianus and his men resumed their march, and toward dusk his scouts came in and reported that the Goths had camped for the night not far away, near the bank of the Maritsa River, whose valley ascends the Rhodope Mountains to the west. Sebastianus silently approached the enemy encampment; he sent part of his men wading upriver through the shallows under the cover of the riverbank, while the others advanced through some thick woods. Then he waited until the middle of the night and attacked. Surprised in their sleep, the Goths were annihilated; this time, there were no prisoners, and all the immense collection of booty that the band had accumulated in the course of a few weeks' raiding was recovered.

This is the only such episode that Ammianus Marcellinus recounted in detail, but Sebastianus probably conducted his harassing operations successfully for some time, while the armies of the two emperors were assembling and beginning to march. As the summer went on, Fritigern and the other Gothic leaders, who were in charge of the fortified camps, must have realized that something was wrong. The country was not as safe as it had been until then: Some bands of young men, sent out for plunder, failed to return; a few outlying, isolated Gothic camps were attacked by surprise and destroyed; and even the influx of booty was beginning to slow down. Even though all the Goths' spies and every deserter reported that Valens's army was still a long way off, Fritigern decided to run no risks: He suspended all raids, called in his roving bands, and ordered all the chiefs to strike the camps.

The Goths dismantled their fortified encampments and started marching through Thrace to gather in the place Fritigern had selected: the city of Cabyle, on the river the Bulgarians today call the Tundzha. There was nothing casual in the choice of this meeting point; it was a centrally located place from which, in case of need, the Gothic horde could retreat toward the Danube under cover of the mountains, strike east to the Black Sea, or return to the south and go back to plundering and daring the Romans to fight. Cabyle—where the wagon-camp grew steadily as more and more groups, including those that had been most widely dispersed, rejoined the main body—was less than sixty miles, following the course of the Tundzha River southward, from Adrianople.

By then, Valens, too, had started to move. The couriers arriving from the East confirmed that Gratian had crushed the barbarian threat on the Rhine and was approaching Thrace with his army. Sebastianus was reporting a series of triumphs, with bands of Goths intercepted and destroyed and much booty recovered. It may be that the general was inclined to exaggerate his accomplishments a little, as Ammianus maliciously observed, but nevertheless he had real successes. Valens, like everyone in his circle, had the feeling that the final phase of the campaign had arrived. They all felt this was the moment for the emperor himself to make his presence felt, conclude the match, and collect the laurels. Gratian, who was little more than a boy, had already won a war; he could surely not be allowed to win another, nor could all the glory of having defeated the Goths redound to the credit of such a useful but disagreeable fellow as Sebastianus. And so Valens left his suburban villa, together with the entire army that had gathered there in the previous weeks, and marched toward the interior of Thrace, resolved to attack the bulk of the enemy forces and destroy them with one blow.

We cannot know for certain how many men made up Valens's army; the hypothetical calculations of historians are rather divergent, but the most credible arrive at a total of around fifteen or twenty thousand. These figures are surprisingly low in comparison to the enormous numbers often quoted by Latin historians for the armies of antiquity. But those figures were largely imaginary, and the reality was much more modest. To assemble twenty thousand men after the losses the Goths had already inflicted on the Romans in nearly two years of war, Valens had been compelled to scrape the bottom of the barrel, leaving only less mobile and less well-trained troops to guard the frontiers. Only on the Euphrates, facing the Persians, had he needed to leave a reasonably substantial deterrent force; but apart from this, the emperor brought with him practically all the line regiments still available in the East, along with all the *scholae*, the cavalry regiments of the imperial guard. Ammianus Marcellinus unequivocally declared this a large army, adding that many veterans had been recalled to service expressly for this campaign. The troops were well paid, and their esprit de corps was still high; without a doubt, they believed they would put a stop to the ragged bands of marauders who had for some time been laying waste the Thracian countryside.

IX

ADRIANOPLE, AUGUST 9, 378

Adrianople was the first great city the emperor came to after his departure from the suburbs of the capital; since Sebastianus's victorious counterraid, however, the Goths had stopped venturing so far, and so Valens decided to press on toward the Rhodope Mountains in the hope of making contact with the enemy. The Goths, too, were moving, marching south from Cabyle as if Fritigern, having been informed that the emperor in person was leading the hunt for him, had decided on a confrontation. Of the two adversaries, the Roman side seemed to be operating more completely in the dark. Although the Romans had a great deal of cavalry, their reconnaissance activities were not very efficient, and at least part of the mounted forces were heavy cavalry, cataphracts or *clibanarii*, as the Romans called them, who fought while enclosed in impenetrable armor and could surely not be wasted in scouting duties. Valens's army had already marched some distance northwest on its way to the mountains where, it was believed, the enemy was still encamped, when some scouting patrols returned and reported that the Goths were much closer than expected: They were coming down the Tundzha river valley behind the Roman column, and there was a chance they might reach the plain and fall on Adrianople.

Fritigern's strategic ability was evident again, as he apparently planned to seal off the road to Constantinople, stop the emperor's supplies from reaching him, and cut off his retreat, thus forcing him to fight on unfavorable ground. Valens, however, grasped the situation and reacted quickly. The Goths were crossing a mountainous region where they had to move comparatively slowly, and it was still possible to block their passage before they completed their outflanking maneuver. Valens sent troops suited for such a mission—light, fast-moving cavalry and archers—and ordered them to occupy the mountain passes the Goths were most likely to traverse. The barbarians, for their part, proceeded with caution, not wishing to expose themselves to a surprise attack in the mountains; they did not try to force the passes, choosing instead a more circuitous route. Their idea was still to descend onto the plain and cut the road to Constantinople, but the Romans had identified their position and the element of surprise was gone. Judging from the reports that reached him in his tent, Valens was unable to determine the exact number of the enemy; he did not know whether he was dealing with the main Gothic army or a detachment that his forces could overwhelm. Finally, he received a report more precise than the others: A scouting party had observed at length the enemy on the march and figured that the Goths had no more than ten thousand men. Valens had more, perhaps even twice as many. He immediately gave orders to turn back to Adrianople, where he planned to attack the Goths as soon as they came out onto the plain.

* * *

Valens's army set up a fortified encampment in the suburbs of Adrianople, complete with ditch and palisade. This was standard practice for the Romans whenever they were in the presence of an enemy, and as it had always worked well for them, no commander would neglect so elementary a precaution. Valens, though, must have felt quite sanguine. The enemy force was advancing toward him, followed at a distance and carefully watched by his scouts; it was weaker than his own; and furthermore, Valens could hope, in a few days, to see the vanguard of Gratian's army emerge from the Maritsa valley. Soon, in fact, one of his nephew's generals arrived in Valens's camp, the same Richomer, commander of the western emperor's imperial guard, who had directed the combined Roman forces at the battle by the Willows. Richomer was carrying a letter from his emperor, in which Gratian promised to appear soon, advised his uncle not to run any risks, and counseled him to wait for his arrival.

This letter from his boy nephew could not have put Valens in a good humor. He convened his war council and asked his generals what should be done. Many of them thought Gratian was right; going it alone would be foolish when waiting a few days would allow the two armies to combine. The leader of the group advocating prudence was the cavalry commander, Victor, a typical representative of the military elite of the time. Victor, too, was the son of immigrants—a Sarmatian, to be exact—and therefore a member of one of the steppe peoples who were, like the Goths, well known for impetuosity. And yet, according to Ammianus, Victor showed no ethnic character traits, and "although a Sarmatian, he was patient and careful." In other words, he was one of those career military officers who had been thoroughly Romanized, even if they might have retained in their physical features and in their accents some foreign traces. For the rest, Victor was a devout and even zealous Catholic who counted among his correspondents such fathers of the church as St. Basil of Caesarea and St. Gregory Nazianzus, and he paid close attention to the theological debates of his time. His Catholicism may have been a reason why the emperor, who was an Arian, had no great love for him. Nevertheless,

Valens knew that Victor was a valuable officer, and the emperor had no intention of depriving himself of such a man's talents.

Buoyed by all the prestige and enthusiasm of his recent victories, Sebastianus lined up on the other side and declared that the imperial army must attack. The courtliest of the generals, those accustomed to gauging the emperor's will before committing themselves, saw at once that Valens wanted to follow Sebastianus's advice. Valens's political position in Constantinople was very weak at that moment; he needed a victory, and did not want to share it with Gratian. And so, in the end, the war council, somewhat heartened by Sebastianus's contagious optimism, decided to attack.

* * *

It was August 8. In Valens's camp just outside Adrianople, word was already spreading that the army would move out the following day, track down the barbarians, and destroy them. While the soldiers were busy polishing weapons and armor and looking after the horses, a group of Goths, sent by Fritigern to parley, presented themselves at the Roman camp. Their leader was a priest: a Gothic priest, evidently, and therefore an Arian, like the emperor. He was carrying a letter from Fritigern requesting negotiations.

The arrival of this diplomatic mission, led by a Christian priest, was an extraordinary moment in the long, complicated history of the cohabitation between Rome and the barbarians. The Goths were in part Christians, but at this point not all of them—and perhaps not even the majority of them—had been converted. The Roman Empire was officially Christian, but in fact it still contained a great many pagans, and hostility toward Christianity was still visible, especially among intellectuals. Those savages who claimed to have been converted to Christianity, with their barbarian priests and their barbarian bishops, were a source of particular irritation to pagans, who lost no opportunity to ridicule them. Ammianus Marcellinus doesn't labor the point, saying only that the Gothic envoy was "a Christian presbyter, as they themselves call such persons." By contrast, our other source, Eunapius, seized the occasion to speak his mind. All the barbarian tribes that had overflowed into the empire, he said, carried with them the idols of their gods and the priests and priestesses of their pagan cults, and they continued to celebrate their ancestral rites. However, Eunapius went on, "they maintain an absolute reserve concerning these matters, over which an impenetrable silence reigns, and they never speak of their mysteries"; in fact, in order to deceive the Romans more completely, they all pretended to be Christians. But this was only a trick, the pagan Greek historian continued: They would dress one man up like a bishop and send him out with all his trappings to deceive the ingenuous; they were prepared to swear on the Bible and on relics oaths that the emperors took seriously, while for them the whole thing was a farce; they could even exhibit a few members of "the tribe of so-called monks," disguised to resemble the monks the Romans had, with their ragged tunics and gray mantles. And yet—and this drove Eunapius crazy—everybody believed them, and the Christians were ready to embrace them as brothers.

Eunapius's version is, of course, open to question. Convinced that Christianity was a collective madness dragging the empire into disaster, he went so far as to make an unfavorable comparison between the Romans' stupidity and the shrewdness of the barbarians, who, he felt, understood how they ought to behave in order to succeed with the enemy but in private continued to practice "sincerely and nobly" their ancestral rites. In reality, the conversion of the Goths to Christianity was anything but farcical, and the above is only the creative description of a pagan writer who bore a grudge against Christians. Nevertheless, it is fascinating to observe that when the Gothic princes decided to send someone to negotiate with Valens, the person they sent was a priest, clearly believing, whether in good or bad faith, that a display of their adherence to Christianity would be the easiest way for them to obtain a hearing with the emperor.

Valens agreed to receive the Gothic envoys and ordered that they be admitted into the camp. Except for the priest, the mission was composed of ordinary people, not high-ranking warriors, a bit of rudeness on the part of the Goths. The priest gave Valens the letter from Fritigern, probably written in either Latin or Greek, because surely there were many among the Goths who knew the languages of the empire. If, on the other hand, the letter was in the Gothic tongue, it would have been written in the alphabet that Ulfila invented for his Gothic Bible, and the priest would have been charged with translating it. We know nothing of this priest, not even his name, but clearly he was a person of importance and one of Fritigern's confidants, because along with the letter the priest carried a secret message from the Gothic commander, to be delivered to the emperor in private.

In the public letter, Fritigern recalled that if he and his people were in Roman territory, it was because they had been admitted as refugees; war and war alone had driven them from their homes and forced them to request asylum. When he granted them permission to cross the Danube and take refuge in the empire, Valens had also promised them land and livestock, Fritigern reminded his readers. Now, asking only that this promise be kept, the Goths were ready to live in peace as faithful subjects of the emperor. The official letter, to which all the Gothic leaders had assented, stopped here. In the secret letter, Fritigern explained that he had always wanted to make peace, but the other chiefs and warriors were full of themselves and would have none of it; however, the letter went on, as soon as the emperor advances with his army and my people realize the power of Rome, they will no doubt calm down, and then an agreement can be negotiated.

We cannot today determine whether or not Fritigern's offer was sincere. A more or less Romanized barbarian leader certainly could have looked forward to excellent career opportunities in the service of the empire, and the proposal contained nothing intrinsically unbelievable. Perhaps the most probable explanation is that Fritigern wished to keep all possibilities open and planned to wait and see how events developed. From a purely military point of view, he was in a fix: The attempt to outflank Valens's army and take up a position between him and his capital had failed. Fritigern's only options were to accept battle in the open field, with everything at stake, or to negotiate; choosing one alternative or the other may well have been difficult for him. In the end, however, the emperor came to the conclusion that he could not trust the letters from Fritigern, and so he sent away the ambassadors and prepared to leave the camp, intending to confront the enemy and see what would happen. After all, whether or not Fritigern was lying, a demonstration of force was necessary to compel the barbarians to submit.

* * *

At dawn on August 9, Valens's army broke camp and started marching toward the Goths' position. The imperial treasury, which always accompanied the emperor's person, and the imperial insignia were brought to a safe place inside the walls of Adrianople, in the custody of the civilian ministers who had followed the sovereign. The army's gear and baggage train, with the supply wagons and the pack animals, remained in the camp, near the city walls, and various units were left there as guards.

The terrain outside Adrianople was hilly, not easy for a marching column to traverse. There was no real road, just a dirt track; the only large Roman road in the area was the Via Egnatia, which started in Constantinople, went through Adrianople, and then continued westward, whereas Valens and his army had to march north to reach the Goths. It was a torrid summer; the land was arid and dry, and the marching troops raised a huge cloud of dust. The army had to cross various small watercourses, but they were all dried up, and the meadow-grass was scorched and turning yellow. The march took the whole morning; at what the Romans called the eighth hour—between one and two in the afternoon—they finally came within sight of the area where the Goths were encamped.

The Roman generals knew very well that the enemy was there, because their mounted scouts had never lost sight of the Goths: They were entrenched, as usual, behind the immense circle formed by their wagons, and outside the ring not a living soul was to be seen. The Goths also knew that the enemy was approaching, not least because of the cloud of dust, and when the Roman vanguard appeared on the horizon, a chorus of shouts, boasts, and insults rose from the wagons, which were filled with hidden warriors.

The exact place where the Goths were encamped and where the battle of Adrianople was fought has never been precisely identified, but some credible hypotheses have been advanced. The site lies in the northwestern corner of European Turkey, not far from the Bulgarian border. At a distance from Adrianople equal to the distance that can be inferred from Ammianus Marcellinus's account, there is a Turkish village called Muratçali. The village is nestled among low hills, which at the time must have been partly cultivated with vineyards and olive groves; a spring still makes the spot ideal for a camp. It would have been easy to defend by deploying the wagon barricade on the surrounding high ground.

Like so many other things, the number of men under Fritigern's command is difficult to pin down. The scouts had counted ten thousand, and historians have generally thought they were mistaken, but perhaps not by very much. Valens clearly had the larger force. But the emperor was ignorant of a crucial fact, namely that the encampment did not contain the entire Gothic army. A great deal of cavalry, together with bands of Alans and Huns, had been sent out to forage elsewhere, and the Roman reconnaissance parties had not spotted them. As long as the barbarians remained closed up in their wagon-circle, they were impossible to count, and so Valens had no reason to change his calculations.

Slowly, methodically, in response to a precise sequence of commands, the Roman infantry began to deploy in order of battle within sight of the wagon-ring, while the cavalry spread out on the flanks and pushed forward, as if to feel and perhaps even encircle the enemy position.

* * *

The exact composition of Valens's army will never be known, because the only document that lists all the regiments of the Roman Empire, both in the East and in the West—a precious and quite famous document known as the *Notitia dignitatum*—was drawn up after the battle of Adrianople, and many regiments wiped out there are probably not included in the list. An educated guess, based on calculated estimates and comparisons between units stationed in the West and those stationed in the East, is that fourteen infantry regiments were destroyed at Adrianople and not subsequently reconstituted.

The modern-sounding term *regiment* is used here in place of *legion*, for the composition of the Roman army had changed a great deal in respect to the army of Rome's classical age. Some units still called themselves legions, but the overwhelming majority of the ancient legions, with the glorious names that went back to the days of Caesar and Augustus—the Ironclad, the Victorious, the Thunderbolt—were scattered in small detachments along the thousands of miles of the imperial border.

The mobile armies, which the emperors kept under their direct control, were made up of two other types of units. One was still called a legion, but it no longer resembled the classical legions, which were actually enormous phalanxes five or six thousand men strong; three or four legions had been enough to constitute a large army. The legions of the late empire, however, were small units, with not more than one thousand men on paper and in reality often fewer, the equivalent of a modern battalion. Alongside the legions were the *auxilia*, which in origin were second-class units, recruited among subjugated barbarian populations; by the time of Adrianople, however, the barbarian recruits were considered the best. *Auxilia* units were much smaller than legions, perhaps no more than a few hundred men. All these units had fanciful names that referred to the arms they carried or the tribes from which they had been recruited or the emperor who had seen to their formation. We know the names of two legions that were with Valens at Adrianople, the Lanciarii or "Spearmen" and the Mattiarii or "Javeliners," as well as the name of one *auxilia* unit, the Batavi, recruited from a Germanic tribe, the Batavians, whose people lived in the Rhine delta. Both the new legions and the *auxilia* had a strong esprit de corps and distinctive insignia, and many of them cultivated their own traditions, which is why modern historians often choose to refer to both kinds of units as *regiments*. Taking into account the loss estimates mentioned above, we can figure that Valens's army at Adrianople comprised a total of perhaps twenty infantry regiments, counting both legions and *auxilia*.

In addition, the Romans had greatly strengthened their cavalry, once the weakest part of the army. It was composed of *scholae*, the cavalry regiments of the imperial guard, as well as regiments of line cavalry with complicated names like Equites Promoti Iuniores and an equally complicated hierarchy of honorific precedence. The size of these regiments is uncertain, but their numbers must have been relatively modest: perhaps five hundred men for each of the prestigious *scholae* and fewer for the others, taking into consideration the enormous cost of cavalry in equipment and remounts. This was an army much different from Julius Caesar's, and not only because the infantry carried spears instead of the classic short swords and fought in a close formation, six or even eight ranks deep, similar to the ancient phalanx of Alexander's Macedonians. By contrast, the heavily armored assault cavalry already looked much like medieval cavalry, with the exception of one decisive detail: The stirrup was unknown to the Romans. There were also many archers, far more than in the past, fighting both on foot and on horseback, as the Asian peoples did. The Roman army, in short, had changed over time, because it constantly had new and different enemies to deal with; but the discipline was the same as in the old days, the traditions were the ancient traditions, the men were battle-hardened veterans, and the morale was high.

* * *

In the early afternoon of August 9, under a sun that was almost directly overhead, the imperial units were massed in perfect order around their dragonlike *draco* standards. They responded to the shouts of the barbarians with the deep lowing of the *barritus*, rhythmically beating their spears against their shields and raising a sinister, threatening din that spread across the plain. On the right wing of the Roman battle array, the cavalry pushed forward and quickly reached the line of high ground where the barbarians' wagon-circle stood. The cavalry on the Roman left wing, which had formed the rear guard of the column on the march, was late in reaching its position but hastening to make up for lost time. The infantry stood lined up in the center: around twenty regimental units, approximately fifteen thousand men. The soldiers of each regiment carried its distinctive insignia painted on their round shields; the insignia of the Lanciarii, for example, was a golden sun on a red background. As soon as the archers had moved within range of the wagon barricade, they started shooting their arrows, more to frighten the enemy than to do him any real damage. And the enemy, in fact, grew frightened; once again, a group of envoys came out from behind the wagons, and they were immediately ushered into the presence of the emperor.

Ammianus Marcellinus was convinced that all the barbarians' offers to negotiate were nothing but ploys to gain time: Fritigern was waiting for the return of his cavalry, which had surely observed the cloud of dust on the horizon and inferred from it that the Roman army was advancing. Once again, Fritigern sent a diplomatic mission made up of ordinary warriors with no one in command; this offended Valens, who said he was still ready to negotiate and offer peace terms, but he insisted on dealing with commanders, the only ones who could guarantee him that the conditions would be respected.

While these discussions went forward, the sun on that torrid August afternoon remained high in the sky. Summer temperatures in those latitudes can reach 104° Fahrenheit, and the Roman soldiers, immobile in their formations, had little to eat and drink. Nothing had been distributed since the morning rations, and the horses, too, were beginning to suffer from thirst. Here and there in the plain, the dry grass caught fire, and the wind blew the acrid smoke toward the Romans; according to Ammianus, the Goths had prepared firewood and other fuel in advance and had set these blazes deliberately. At last, their envoys agreed to return to Fritigern and explain to him that the emperor was ready for negotiations, but he wanted the meeting to be a parley between leaders.

It is not at all clear why Valens let himself be persuaded to negotiate, having left Adrianople resolved to put an end to the barbarian problem once and for all. Perhaps the sight of the enormous mass of wagons convinced the emperor that the enemy was stronger than he had been led to believe, or perhaps he followed the old conditioned reflex of every Roman ruler of this period, in which the empire had a desperate need of able-bodied men: There, in those wagons, was a precious source of manpower, sturdy fellows who could immediately be inducted into the army or sent to cultivate the vast latifundia of the Roman state, as had happened a few months previously with the Taifali prisoners of war, deported to Italy and successfully settled in the Po plain. With the Goths practically in his hands, perhaps slaughtering the lot of them seemed like a waste.

Fritigern, having been informed that Valens was prepared to parley, but only with the Gothic chieftains, sent back a response: He would come to the talks in person, but he wanted the Romans to turn over a high-ranking hostage so the Goths could be sure there would be no dirty tricks. Considering Fritigern's earlier, miraculous escape from Lupicinus's banquet, at which the Romans had very nearly done him in, his caution does not seem unreasonable, and in any case, this additional delay is insufficient grounds to be sure that he was already planning treachery. Valens and his advisers saw nothing wrong; when a Gothic warrior returned to report Fritigern's condition, they immediately began discussing who should be chosen to go to the Gothic camp as a hostage.

At first, Valens proposed to send a relative of his, Equitius, a high-ranking official who was then master of the imperial palace. The others, probably relieved not to have been chosen themselves, quickly supported the emperor's proposal. But Equitius had once been a prisoner of the Goths, and although he had managed to escape, he carried such a memory of the experience that no one, not even the emperor, could persuade him to go back to them. Then the Frankish commander of the western emperor's imperial guard, Richomer, said that he would go, permitting himself a sarcastic word or two to the effect that in circumstances like these, you could tell which men had guts and which did not, and adding that since he was ready to risk his neck to serve his emperor, whether he did so as a hostage or on the battlefield made no difference to him. Nevertheless, Richomer needed some time to get ready; he had to bring with him proofs of his rank and of his family origins in the Frankish nobility, because otherwise the wary Goths might have believed the emperor had sent them a common fellow disguised as a great personage.

Obviously, any mutual trust that may have existed between the adversaries was long gone. Right up to the end, however, one has the impression that at least on the Roman side, everyone was genuinely trying to facilitate matters and to arrive at a peaceful accord. Our source for this story is, as usual, Ammianus Marcellinus; if we had an account written by a Gothic priest, the affair might well appear in a totally different light. Regardless, it was now late afternoon, and the Romans, who had been under arms since dawn and had eaten nothing all day, were still beating on their shields and threatening the enemy with whatever strength remained in their throats. Richomer departed on horseback to present himself at the Gothic camp as a hostage, anticipating that the negotiations would be able to begin in earnest.

* * *

When Count Richomer rode out of the Roman battle formation, with only a few hours of daylight left, everyone, at least on the Roman side, must have been sure that, at least for that day, the battle was postponed. The Goths had repeatedly requested a parley, and Valens, thanks to Fritigern's secret letter, was certain that their chieftains were sincere. The Gothic warriors would have to be convinced, because no one likes to surrender, but the emperor could offer generous conditions, and the princes would explain to their men that they had no other choice.

At this time, the Goths were no longer hunkered down behind their wagon barricade. As soon as the Romans lined up in battle order a few hundred yards away from them, the warriors had come out and taken up positions on the high ground in front of the wagons. This was the nomads' typical way of doing battle: The wagon-circle served as a fortified camp, a safe place for their women and their booty, and a refuge they could fall back on and defend should things go wrong, but the actual battle was fought outside the ring, in the open field, and the defenders' objective was, in fact, to keep the enemy as far away from the wagons as possible.

Protected by their wooden shields, the Goths withstood the first harassing shots of the Roman archers without suffering much damage. When the negotiations were in the works, their tension must have relaxed a little, though obviously everyone remained on the alert. And then, suddenly, the situation came to a head. Apparently, the guard cavalry, the select Scutarii regiments, who should have shown more discipline, first broke ranks. Probably a squadron or two had pushed too far forward, and the Goths were afraid of a treacherous attack, and certainly the mounted archers who accompanied the cavalry found themselves facing such inviting targets that they were unable to resist the temptation and started shooting arrows again.

The commander of the Scutarii was named Bacurius; he was one of the many foreign officers in the imperial army, a prince from the Caucasus who later made a fine career for himself but who, at least on this occasion, did not know how to keep his men in line. Here and there the riders of the guard urged their horses so far forward they could almost nuzzle the enemy, and finally the barbarians, tired of such provocations, rushed the Romans en masse. The Roman cavalry and archers, taken by surprise, retreated in disorder, under the eyes of the soldiers of both armies. It had been only a localized incident, but it was enough to make everyone tense again: Richomer, about to reach the enemy camp, realized that proceeding at that particular moment really would mean risking his neck, and he turned back. The negotiating process had not yet really begun but at this point it was dead and buried.

* * *

The two armies stood facing each other, and on both sides the men were tired and tense after an entire day spent in an alternation of hope and disappointment. At that precise moment, completely unexpectedly—at least as far as the Romans were concerned—the Gothic, Hunnish, and Alan cavalry, which had ridden off a few days previously to forage, emerged amid the hills. The horsemen had probably come down the course of the Tundzha River, whose waters could not have been much more than six inches deep in that dry season, and therefore the barbarian cavalry had raised no dust. By riding down the bed of the deeply embanked river, they had been able to come up close to the Roman lines before anyone noticed them. Seeing the Goths massed in defense of their wagon-circle and in front of them the Romans in battle array, the barbarian cavalry immediately charged. The horsemen crashed into the Roman cavalry, which had been brought forward to cover the left wing, and in an instant the dust of the fray rose so high it hid everything.

The Roman cavalry, taken by surprise, retreated until it was almost on top of the infantry. But the infantry ranks were solid and the soldiers professionals, and they held steady. Supported by the infantry's shouts of encouragement, the cavalry stopped falling back, managed to reorganize, and returned to the fight. Some cavalry units, probably once again belonging to the imperial guard, which was made up of select troops and had heavier equipment and better horses, overwhelmed the enemy riders in front of them. Their impact drove the Goths back, and there, on the left wing, elements of the Roman cavalry managed to advance all the way to the wagon barricade.

Meanwhile, the two masses of infantry had made contact all along the line: two hordes of ironclad men, shouting and trying to crush the enemy or hurl him back with the weight of their shields, plying their swords or spears through the spaces between one shield and another, while the archers and slingers—the Romans deployed behind the line of heavy infantry and the Goths posted on the wagon barricade—loosed their missiles at point-blank range.

Had there been any reserve troops, or had the generals been capable of making any sort of decision amid the wild confusion of a battle started almost by chance, the Roman cavalry's counterattack on the left wing could have been supported, the wagon-ring broken through, the Goths put to rout. Instead, exactly the opposite happened. At some point, the Roman cavalry units that had driven back the enemy and reached the Gothic wagons realized to their horror that no one was following them. In fact, after the combat fragmented into innumerable individual duels, the rest of the Roman cavalry had been overcome, and the Gothic and Alan cavalry then turned back, taking the leading Roman units in the flank and rear. In an instant, the armored cavalry regiments that had fought the hardest and advanced the farthest were overthrown by the enemy cavalry, crushed against the wagon barricade and cut to pieces in a chaos of dead and mutilated men and horses.

* * *

An ancient army always formed up for battle with the infantry in the center and the cavalry on the wings; ordinarily, cavalry was limited and all its energies were spent in fighting the cavalry of the enemy, so the infantry could fight its battle almost without worrying about its mounted adversaries.The worst disasters in Roman military history coincided with the rare cases in which the Romans faced an enemy with a preponderant force of cavalry that subsequently surrounded them: This is what happened at Cannae against Hannibal, and the same thing occurred at Carrhae, in Mesopotamia, when Crassus, the rival of Caesar and Pompey, was defeated and killed by the Parthians. By the time of Adrianople, the imperial army had expanded and prepared its mounted forces with the specific aim of fighting effectively against enemies who had a great deal of cavalry and knew how to use it. And yet, at least at Adrianople, not even this was enough: The barbarians had too many riders, and above all, they appeared on the battlefield by surprise, with all the advantages of the moment and the terrain. In the end, the Roman cavalry was swept away "as if by the collapse of a great rampart."

And then the situation at Cannae presented itself again: The infantry, which was advancing laboriously, and uphill, toward the wagons, suddenly saw that the enemy cavalry was about to fall on its flank and rear. Instinctively, the men began to back up and huddle together, trying to get away from the danger, until they formed a single mass covered by their shields.

"The foot-soldiers," Ammianus Marcellinus wrote, "stood in the open, their companies so crowded together that hardly one of them could pull out his sword or draw back his arm. The clouds of rising dust blotted out the sky, which resounded with ghastly cries." The Gothic and Hunnish archers shot their arrows into the mass, but they couldn't do much damage to soldiers wearing armor and covered by their big wooden shields; therefore, after a while the barbarian cavalry rode in among them, confident of trampling them and cutting them to pieces. But the Roman infantry was made up of veterans determined to sell their lives dearly; every time the cavalry charged, the mass of infantry closed ranks and stood firm. However, their resistance could not last forever. The infantry was trained to fight in close order with the spear, but after such a long battle, most of the spears were broken, and the soldiers were left with only the sword, not the proper weapon for fighting cavalry. Their shields, too, which were fashioned from wooden planks, eventually fell to pieces, riddled as they were with enemy arrows. Weary, tormented by thirst and heat, and fighting on terrain slippery with blood, where they trod on their dead and wounded comrades, the Romans repulsed another charge, and then another, and finally reached the moment when the majority of them lost their nerve and started running away.

* * *

After the cavalry of the imperial guard was routed, Valens had found himself practically alone with his generals. When he saw that the battle was lost, he took refuge in the midst of the infantry regiments that were maintaining a modicum of cohesion and trying to retreat in good order, namely the Lanciarii and the Mattiarii. Victor, the Sarmatian cavalry commander, went to the regiment of Batavian *auxilia* that had been left in reserve and tried to persuade them to move forward with him so they could reach the emperor and bring him to safety, but the Batavians understood all too well what was happening; they refused to follow Victor, and then they too ran away. Victor decided that he had done enough for one day and concentrated his efforts on saving his own skin.

Many other generals, realizing that the day was lost, cleared off, and since they had good horses and the men in their escorts were well paid, they made it to safety. Among them were Richomer, who a few hours earlier had offered himself as a hostage so peace negotiations could get under way, and Saturninus, who had commanded operations against the Goths in the Balkans the previous year. But whoever had no horse had no hope. In the battles of antiquity, this was the moment in which the defeated side suffered the greatest losses, and the battle of Adrianople was no exception. As long as there was a little light left in the sky, the Goths pursued the runaways, massacring all they could catch, without giving any quarter either to those who surrendered or to those who tried to resist. Fortunately for the Romans, when the rout began it was already nearly dark, and the pursuit couldn't last long, because it was a moonless night. But the great majority of the veteran soldiers of the army of the East remained on the battlefield where they had fallen, and many of their generals fell there, too, including Trajanus, who had commanded the first operations against the Goths two years before, and Sebastianus, who had fought against them with such success during the last few months. Some of the highest functionaries of the emperor's court were killed, men such as Valerianus, master of the imperial stables, and Equitius, master of the palace, he who a few hours earlier had refused to be sent to the barbarians as a hostage because it was too dangerous. Thirty-five senior officers fell, both regimental commanders and imperial staff officers, along with two-thirds of the veterans that Valens had brought together from all the garrisons of the empire.

As for Valens, no more was ever heard of him. He was probably struck by an arrow while in the midst of the soldiers, when it was already dark, because otherwise someone would have noticed; however, Ammianus was not surprised that he was not identified later, because after the battle some Goths roamed over the field for several days, stripping the bodies, and when the local farming people finally dared to come forward to bury all those dead, the emperor's corpse must have been unrecognizable. Sometime later, however, a more tragic story circulated through the empire, a story that Ammianus dutifully recorded, even though he did not seem to consider it credible. According to this version, the wounded Valens sought shelter in some rural building, a farmhouse or a tower, together with his bodyguards and a few of the palace eunuchs who had been unwilling to abandon him. When the barbarians arrived, the Romans barricaded themselves inside and refused to surrender. Perhaps the enemy might have ignored them and passed on, but someone on the upper floor of the building started shooting arrows, and with that the infuriated Goths gathered bundles of straw and firewood, set fire to the house, and burned alive everyone inside, including the emperor.

X

AFTER THE DISASTER

The news of the defeat at Adrianople and the death of Valens caused a huge emotional reaction throughout the Roman Empire. This reaction was not, however, chiefly attributable to the shocking fact that a Roman emperor had been killed while fighting barbarians. Such a calamity had occurred before; in the preceding century, the emperor Decius had fallen in battle against none other than the Goths, who even back then were sending large raiding parties into the Balkans, and a few years later another emperor, Valerianus, had been defeated and captured by the Persians and had died an ignominious death as their prisoner (according to persistent rumors, the enemy sovereign had used the emperor as a stool for mounting his horse). More than a hundred years had passed since then, so not even the very old could recall so momentous a disaster as Adrianople; all the same, however, there were good reasons not to treat the death of an emperor in battle as a rare event. The empire had known many a general who had seized power and proclaimed himself emperor and reigned until another general challenged him; those who lost usually were killed and passed into history as usurpers, but as long as they were alive they were revered by their subjects as legitimate emperors. In practice, the sacredness of the emperor was a fiction; it was the office that was sacred, not the man. The purple and the diadem were sacred, not the body that temporarily wore them.

Other reasons, therefore, caused the emotion aroused by the news from Adrianople. For two years, public opinion had followed, with bated breath, the tragedy unfolding in the Balkan provinces. People learned a little about it from the dribbles of news released by the imperial palace and much more from rumors, whispers, and urban legends. The ancestral fear of the barbarians, which always lurked in a corner of the Roman consciousness, suddenly awoke. Fear can be a powerful sensation, and the news arriving from the regions devastated by the Goths was tailor-made to intensify it; one need only consider the somewhat macabre avidity with which the writers of the time, including Ammianus Marcellinus, lingered over the most hair-raising and exciting stories, describing the cruelty of the barbarians, detailing what they did to their prisoners, what they did to women. The public followed all this breathlessly, with excitement heightened by the knowledge that those horrors were going on close to them, within the empire, and that if the situation got only a little worse, such things could happen to them, too.

The emperor had bestirred himself at last and marched out with the flower of the army, one ironclad, glinting regiment after the other, to have done with the problem once and for all, and everyone had taken it for granted that the barbarians were finally going to get what was coming to them; the empire's manifest destiny, after all, was to defeat its enemies. Instead, the unthinkable had happened, and this news provoked a general trauma all over the empire.

Another reason why the news about Adrianople elicited such a profound emotional reaction is connected to the controversial character of Valens. When the public learned that he had been defeated, and especially that his body had no doubt remained on the battlefield, people had conflicting reactions: dismay, certainly, because the man was, after all, the emperor, but also a kind of grim satisfaction. Many were ready to say they had long known Valens was headed for disaster sooner or later. Ammianus Marcellinus went so far as to open his account of the war against the Goths by describing the ominous signs that had presaged Valens's death, signs—according to Ammianus—that proliferated throughout the empire as soon as people found out about the arrival of the Goths. Naturally, these too were urban legends; the ancients were sincerely convinced that great events, in particular great misfortunes or the deaths of illustrious men, were foreshadowed by portents and miracles, and after a catastrophe occurred, everyone was certain that the signs had indeed been there for all to see.

The passage in which Ammianus Marcellinus describes the omens foreshadowing the disaster at Adrianople and Valens's death makes fascinating reading. In the first place, it vividly evokes how superstitious the Romans were, with a degree of superstition we tend to associate with the Middle Ages, but which was deeply rooted in the mentality of the ancients; second, it gives an idea of the climate created as the news spread through the empire, when after the fact all were prepared to say that Valens had been bound to come to a bad end. Ammianus provides an astonishing list, including detailed prognostications from soothsayers as well as auguries foretelling the disaster: howling wolves, lugubriously singing night-birds, even the sun, which rose paler than usual.

Moreover, sometime before Adrianople, Valens had had the king of Armenia killed by treachery, and on another occasion he had condemned one of his ministers to death with an accusation of treason that was probably of his own invention. This climate of dread was normal under the empire, and rare indeed was the emperor who did not have the occasional political trial and the odd murder on his conscience; but after Valens's death, word began to spread that the ghosts of those whom he had had unjustly killed had appeared, gnashing their teeth and whispering funeral dirges that could make hair stand on end.

Other auguries abounded. Not far from Constantinople, a dead cow was found with its throat slit, and for some ungraspable reason the thing was considered a portent of widespread public mourning; and workers recovering old stones for reuse in a new construction found one incised with Greek verses of great antiquity, which foretold the Gothic invasion. But the most interesting of the omens Ammianus recorded is this: "In Antioch," he said, "it had become customary, in the brawls and riots of the common people, for whoever thought himself wronged to cry out unrestrainedly, 'Let Valens burn alive!' " This detail provides convincing proof that stories of this type started to circulate only after the battle, after everyone had heard the legend—likewise unverified and unverifiable—according to which Valens had burned alive in a farmhouse.

* * *

The Roman world was full of superstition, with a blind belief in soothsayers and portents. And yet this was also the society that was slowly but surely spreading the Christian message, although it had soon found a way to divide over the meaning of that message. Valens, as we know, was a Christian, but in that period one had to choose either the Arian or the Catholic confession. The competition was ferocious, and it split the community in half. More was at stake than prevailing in public opinion and winning over the majority of the faithful; the physical possession of ecclesiastical buildings was also in play, along with the administration of the properties attached to them, which were enormous. Valens stood with the Arians and never made a mystery of his preference; when a decision had to be made as to whether a basilica would be run by Arian priests or Catholic priests, the emperor regularly intervened in favor of the Arians. So Catholics had little trust in him, and in the great cities with large Catholic communities—including the capital, Constantinople—he was roundly hated. We can therefore imagine the reaction of the Catholic world to Valens's death, to the fact that he had died so wretchedly, and that—the crowning irony—he had died at the hands of barbarians who were, in part, heretics like him.

Christians disapproved of soothsayers and portents, which at least officially belonged to the pagan tradition, even though, in reality, everyone believed in them; but predictions made by holy men and containing a moral lesson were a totally different matter. After Adrianople, a story spread among people in Catholic circles: When Valens was about to depart from Constantinople on his way to confront the Goths, Isaac, a holy monk, a man who spoke truth even to the powerful and was afraid of nothing, had presented himself to the emperor and addressed him approximately as follows: "Behold, this is the moment to stop defending heretics and persecuting the orthodox; restore to the Catholics the churches you confiscated from them and gave to their enemies, and victory shall be yours." The emperor took offense and ordered that the monk be arrested and imprisoned until such time as he, Valens, should return, and then the emperor would decide how to punish him. But the monk replied, "If you don't restore the churches, you shall not return."

How much truth there may be in this story is difficult to say, but upon learning that Valens would not be returning, the Catholics began promoting the Isaac anecdote as if it were the Gospel. At this point, the death of the emperor became a judgment of God. St. Ambrose, the bishop of Milan, addressed Gratian, the emperor of the West, guaranteeing him that God would give him the victory against the Goths, whom the saint compared to the biblical nations of Gog and Magog. The orthodox faith, in short, guaranteed the victory, while Valens's ruin was a just punishment for the persecutions he had inflicted on Catholics.

It would be interesting to know how the Arians reacted to all this. At the time, they may even have represented the majority faith in a large part of the eastern empire, but we are ignorant of their reaction and will forever remain so, because very few texts propounding the Arian point of view ever had a chance of coming down to us. However, we do know how the pagans reacted: Inevitably, they accused the new religion of having provoked the anger of the gods and deprived the empire of their protection. Let them not come and tell us, thundered Libanius the rhetorician, that the generals were bunglers or the soldiers cowardly; we should rather celebrate the memory of their struggle, the courage with which they shed their blood and died at their posts. Their valor was equal to that of their forebears, and for love of glory they put up with heat and thirst, fire and sword, and preferred death to dishonor. "If the enemy defeated them," the old Greek concluded, "I am convinced that the cause was the gods' anger against us."

* * *

The battle of Adrianople was clearly a trauma for the ancient world. Ammianus Marcellinus decided to close his work with an account of that battle, because the symbolic value of Adrianople seemed conclusive to him; as for what would follow, he said, let some other, younger writer record it if he chose. But for Ammianus, the history of the Roman Empire finished there, as if it had come to a full stop.

Modern historians have been all too inclined to adopt this point of view. Symbolic dates, those that clearly mark the end of one era and the beginning of another, are notably rare in history, and the authors of the last few centuries, those who have shaped our image of the ancient world and the Middle Ages, saw immediately that Adrianople had all the characteristics required to be a date of this kind: It was the starting point of a crisis that would eventually end with the disappearance of the Western Roman Empire. Before Adrianople, the empire had known many disasters, but it had always recovered from them. After the barbarian invasions and the civil wars of the third century, great emperors, including Diocletian and Constantine the Great, had come to power, and such men continued to be part of the Roman Empire's great history. But after Adrianople, it seemed possible to declare that history over. If anything, a new one was beginning, one the historians found very much less gratifying: the history of the Byzantine Empire.

But historians have considered Adrianople a decisive turning point for another reason, and in this case, the impulse came more from imagination than analysis. One could see in this battle the triumph of cavalry—which prefigured the medieval period—over infantry, the incarnation of ancient Rome. Adrianople can look like the legions' last battle and the end of the Roman army, which after that disaster was never the same, and like the arrival not only of a new way of fighting but also of a whole new universe of values and symbols, barbarian in origin, that can be set against the universe of the ancients.

Yet dramatic interpretations of this sort—what might be called the "clash of civilizations" reading of history—do not stand up very well under close examination. The Roman army was too large an organism to die in a single battle; in fact, it kept on fighting for several centuries, and did so rather well. Besides, it was already changing of its own accord. To imagine a radical difference between the two armies of Valens and Fritigern, identifying the former with the Roman past and the latter with the medieval future, is to believe that Rome and the barbarians were two separate realities utterly unconnected with each other. In reality, the two armies were almost identical, constituted in more or less the same way and armed with the same weapons. Nonetheless, even without overstating the impact of Adrianople, we can say that its consequences were deep and their significance enormous, albeit deserving of a little more credit for complexity than they usually receive.

* * *

The morning after the battle, the Goths began to appreciate the extent of their victory. If Emperor Valens's body really did remain unidentified among the heaps of the slain and was never found again, perhaps the barbarians did not realize they had killed him until sometime later, but they knew that the Roman army that had marched against them the previous day no longer existed. There were so many of the fallen enemy that the Goths did not bother to despoil them all, and more than enough weapons and armor than they would need to rearm their whole force. In general, barbarian peoples stopped where they were after such a victory, sometimes even for a long while, to celebrate, to perform religious rites, or simply because they had no other plans, no idea of how to go on. But the Goths had been in contact with the Roman world for a long time, they were learning fast, and their princes, especially Fritigern, had a strategic vision of the situation. And so that very morning, instead of remaining near the battlefield, the Goths started marching toward the city of Adrianople.

They had already laid siege to Adrianople once in the past, without success, an experience that elicited a famous remark from their leader then, to the effect that Goths should not make war on walls. But this time they had a precise reason for returning to the city: The Goths had learned from traitors and deserters that the members of the *consistorium*, the emperor's ministers, had stayed behind in Adrianople, along with the imperial insignia and, best of all, Valens's treasury. This clearly made the place worth another try, and Ammianus Marcellinus only employed a commonplace when he described the barbarians as they headed for Adrianople, resolved to destroy it, "like wild animals made more ferocious by the exciting smell of blood." Actually, they were not acting like wild beasts at all; the move they were making was perfectly rational.

By ten in the morning, the barbarians were there already, which means that they had left early and moved very fast. The city had barred its gates, but all the soldiers and servants whom Valens had left there the previous day had spent the night in the camp outside the city walls. The municipal government would not let them in, suspicious as the magistrates were about the security of their city. The soldiers, therefore, had entrenched themselves in their camp by the walls, and there they met the Goths' attack. The combat around Adrianople went on for several hours, and at some point a large group of Roman soldiers—Ammianus said three hundred—all deserted together and went over to the enemy. Three hundred men were practically a regiment, and one is struck by the ease with which mass desertions like this could take place in an army that had too many regiments recruited almost completely from within a single tribal group. This particular mass desertion, however, ended very badly, because the Goths—perhaps indeed excited, in this case, by the smell of blood—opened their ranks to let the deserters pass and then killed them all. From that moment on, Ammianus said, no Roman soldier, not even those in desperate situations, gave another thought to deserting.

The combat around the walls of Adrianople went on for several hours, while the sky gradually clouded up and then turned dark, until, luckily for the defenders, a violent, torrential downpour arrived, a summer storm complete with thunder and lightning, and the Goths, perhaps out of superstitious fright more than anything else, broke the siege and retreated to the refuge of their wagons. But there was a great deal left of the day, and while their warriors were eating and caring for their wounds and contusions, the Gothic chieftains sent an envoy with an ultimatum for the city fathers: If the inhabitants wanted to save their lives, they must open the gates and surrender. This messenger, however, didn't dare enter the city, for fear the Romans would do away with him. The ultimatum alone was brought inside and read to the Roman commanders, but everyone decided to pay it no heed.

Then the Goths had recourse to another stratagem: They sent a new delegation, this one made up of Roman officers who had deserted (they, too!) the previous day and gone over to the barbarians.

These men were supposed to present themselves at the gates of the city and try to gain admittance by declaring that they had been captured by the enemy but had escaped from the Gothic camp and now wanted to return to their comrades.

Ammianus's account at this point seems to be nothing but a report of desertions, of Romans going over to the Goths, and in this instance, the deserters weren't simple soldiers; they were *candidati*, members of a select group of officers who served as a kind of personal guard for the emperor and at the same time formed a breeding ground for future staff officers destined for top-rank military careers. Naturally, there were many barbarians among the *candidati*, too; in one of St. Jerome's books, the *Life of St. Hilarion*, one of these officers, a *candidatus*, Frankish by nationality, had been sent on a mission to Syria. He had red hair and milk-white skin, spoke Latin and Frankish, but not Greek or Syriac, and he surely must have looked fairly exotic to indigenous eyes. But the fact that several *candidati* deserted at Adrianople and went over to the barbarians is genuinely astounding, and gives us a measure of the army's plunging morale at the moment of the catastrophe.

These high-ranking deserters had been ordered by their new masters to set fires after they got inside the city walls; the plan was to occupy the citizenry and soldiers in extinguishing the fires so that the besiegers could seize the opportunity and come bursting in.

When the *candidati* approached the ditches, stretching out their hands and shouting that they were Romans, the unsuspecting sentries let them pass into the city; however, once the *candidati* were inside, they were taken to offices and questioned. The men questioning them realized their statements contradicted one another too much, whereupon the city magistrates put them to the torture. In the later Roman Empire, the torturers were professionals, so in the end the deserters confessed their treason and were all duly beheaded.

Inside Adrianople, the citizens expected the Goths to attack again the following day and were feverishly at work reinforcing the defenses.

They barricaded the gates with great boulders; built mounds of earth and stones against the weakest sections of the walls, mounted war engines on the glacis and in the towers, and collected a reserve supply of water, because the previous day, while fighting in the heat, many soldiers had suffered from thirst and a couple had even died of dehydration. The Goths, in fact, attacked that night, hoping to gain advantage from surprise, but the defenses were already complete, and not only the soldiers but also the citizenry and even the imperial court attendants fought on the ramparts. In Adrianople, there was, among other things, a big arsenal, a state-owned arms factory, with a workforce made up of workers who knew how to use weapons as well as to make them, so the civilian population was able to collaborate effectively in the city's defense. When the assailants thronged around the city gates, trying to break them in, they were met with a hail of arrows and stones, and the war machines flung massive rocks at them. For their part, the Goths shot arrows at the ramparts incessantly and made a great effort to demolish the walls. The battle raged during the last hours of the night and into the next day, but the barbarians' attacks grew steadily weaker and in the end stopped altogether; once again, the Goths had to acknowledge that taking a fortified city without siege machinery was impossible.

In attacks of this kind, casualties were always high, and the Goths began to lose heart; after all, the Romans had always considered the inclination to get discouraged easily a barbarian characteristic, while civilized men were the ones who set a goal and pursued it obstinately, without letting themselves be discouraged by failures. The Goths returned to their camp and treated their wounds, Ammianus said, "with their tribal medicine." He seems rather skeptical about its efficacy, even though, as a matter of fact, Roman medicine was hardly more reassuring. But what chiefly occupied the Goths was quarreling among themselves, accusing one another of having forgotten Fritigern's instructions. Some started to say that besieging the city was a mistake, and that they would have done better to resume plundering the still-rich countryside. Ammianus confirmed that deserters and fugitives had described certain areas house by house, including the very interiors of the richest ones, and we can imagine that fugitive slaves guided the barbarians to their masters' homes with particular relish. So in the end, the Goths decided to let Adrianople be and returned to scourging the province.

Meanwhile, no one among the Romans could say for certain what had happened to Valens. As soon as the barbarians lifted the siege, all the courtiers, functionaries, and eunuchs who had been besieged in Adrianople left the city, traveling at night and on side roads, and took refuge in Illyricum and Macedonia, where they were careful to secure the imperial treasury. They were still convinced that their emperor would turn up there, at the head of the troops that had survived the catastrophe; it would take a while for them to realize they would never see him again.

* * *

Uncertainty reigned in the capital as well. The Goths were not far away, and even though everyone knew that barbarians had never yet successfully stormed a walled city, the fear they inspired was magnified by recent events. One can imagine the panic that gripped the citizens of Constantinople when the news reached them that the barbarians, having pillaged all the surrounding countryside and killed or enslaved the majority of the rural population, were approaching. The attraction of the riches concentrated in the metropolis was too great to ignore. They moved quite cautiously, as if they did not really believe the Roman army had been eliminated. Having experienced disasters in the past, they were always fearful of surprise attacks when they were on the march. At last, however, they reached Constantinople and camped outside the walls.

Some troops had remained in the capital, but not enough to sally forth and give battle; the most the Roman commanders could hope for was to distract the enemy by conducting harassing operations against him, and they had on hand exactly the right troops for this sort of action, namely some units of Arab cavalry—Saracens, as they were called at the time—stationed in the capital. The Roman army recruited mercenaries in the most distant lands, and Arabs were not particularly exotic: Some were subjects of the empire, and Christians, and other nomadic Arabs had had treaties with Rome for many years. These tribes furnished mercenaries (as in this case) and escorted caravans on behalf of the Romans. The army that Valens had gathered for the war against the Goths included troops of Arab cavalry, some of which may well have fought at Adrianople and been destroyed there, but at least one unit had stayed in the capital. Ammianus Marcellinus remarked that they were not worth very much in a pitched battle, but raiding was in their blood, and in fact Roman generals used them chiefly for scouting and long-range expeditions, for searching out supplies and forage. This time, however, as a unit of Goths was approaching too close to the city walls, the Saracens were sent out to attack them; during the hand-to-hand combat, one of them overcame his Gothic foe, slit his throat with his knife, applied his mouth to the wound, and drank his blood.

We have no idea of the ritual or magical significance this gesture may have had for the Bedouins, but the Goths were cowed by it: These long-haired madmen who fought practically naked, uttered bloodcurdling shrieks, and drank their enemies' blood were decidedly too barbaric for a partly Romanized and Christianized people like the Goths. From that moment, Ammianus said, their courage began to fail; they beheld the immensity of the walls that defended Constantinople, and behind the walls the blocks of houses, many stories high, that seemed to extend as far as the eye could see. In the end, discouraged by the capital's vastness, they renounced the siege and retreated. At least for the moment, they were fated to find in the great cities of the empire a prey beyond their strength to bring down.

XI

THEODOSIUS

Following Valens's defeat and death, the empire's government of the East, closely identified with the person of the emperor, ceased to exist. The ministers and the insignia of power and even the imperial treasury had traveled with Valens wherever he went, and all those people and riches were scattered, fleeing through the Balkan Mountains. No authority in Constantinople was capable of assuming power, even if only provisionally, and for once no general decided to take advantage of the situation by usurping the throne.

Only in the West were there an emperor and a government. In fact, there were two emperors: Gratian, who was a young man of nineteen, and his little brother Valentinian II. As soon as Gratian learned of the enormity of the Roman defeat and the death of his uncle, he and his army retraced their steps in great haste and took up positions in Illyricum, resolved to defend the empire should the barbarians come their way. It was up to Gratian and his ministers to choose a new emperor of the eastern empire, and they needed a few months to find the right candidate, but in January 379, Theodosius, one of Gratian's generals, was, with the consent of the army, proclaimed emperor of the East.

Much the same process had occurred when Valens was nominated: First the army of the West acclaimed Valentinian, and only afterward did he decide to appoint his younger brother to govern in the East. From a political point of view, the East was indeed the younger brother of the West, for several reasons: The empire had been born in the West, Rome was in the West, the richest senators were those from the West; the western units of the army traditionally contained the most seasoned warriors, and they were also the ones that most easily succeeded in imposing their candidates for the imperial throne. Moreover, the West was synonymous with Latin, and Latin was still the language of the army and the law. But Easterners were starting to reject this status of political minority; for some time, they had known that theirs was the most populous, wealthiest, and most civilized part of the empire. Constantine had simply recognized that fact when he transferred the capital to the shores of the Bosporus. In the dissatisfaction that the Greek East felt at the political and military hegemony of the Latin West lay the seeds of competition—if not hostility—between the two parts of the Roman Empire; those seeds would not fail to produce fruit, and soon.

* * *

Theodosius is the last great protagonist of this story: the man who, in the years after Adrianople, worked harder than anyone else to fill the breach and redress the situation as far as possible.

Like almost all emperors, Theodosius was a career army officer; he came from the Far West, from Spain, and he was only thirty-two years old, but he already had experience to spare. His father, Theodosius the Elder, had been Rome's most famous general in the days of Valentinian and had fought in half the world, from Britain to Africa. His son had grown up accompanying him on his various campaigns until, at a very early age—twenty-six or twenty-seven—he was appointed governor of one of the frontier provinces. At the time, Theodosius, a young man with all the right connections, seemed destined for swift promotion and a brilliant career; but in the Roman Empire, careers sometimes ended suddenly and badly. Valentinian started to mistrust Theodosius the Elder, who was too popular with his soldiers, exactly the type of general who might attempt a coup d'état, and so the emperor relieved him of his command and subjected him to a political trial. Then Valentinian died, but his sons, likewise unwilling to keep so awkward a man as Theodosius the Elder on their hands, had him condemned to death and executed. His son was spared on condition that he retire to private life, and he had gone to live on his estates in Spain.

All this had happened in 376. Two years later, Gratian found himself obliged to choose a candidate to rule the eastern empire, one with shoulders broad enough to bear up under a frightful load. Moreover, the emperor's choice had to be popular with the army, otherwise, Gratian's own throne might begin to wobble. His selection of Theodosius, who met these requirements, quickly proved to be an astute move. Theodosius was cruel when necessary, but he had a political sensibility; he knew how to accept compromise when it was inevitable, but he also knew how to solve a problem at its root when he thought the situation required it. For example, he brutally simplified the religious question. When named emperor, he was not yet even a Christian, but he quickly got himself baptized and lined up with the Catholics, not the Arians. As Arianism was almost unknown in the West, this was probably an obligatory choice for a Westerner, but Theodosius drew political conclusions from it. The new emperor would put an end once and for all to the religious disputes which sowed discord among his subjects and which, in Valens's time, had weakened the very authority of the emperor; he would no longer allow these theological arguments, so typical of Greek intellectuals, to split the East. One year after taking power, Theodosius published an edict three lines long, in which he decreed that his subjects were bound to follow the only true religion, namely Catholicism. All other Christian sects were stripped of their authority; they could no longer possess religious buildings or practice their faith in public, and should anyone object, not only would God punish him in the next life, but the state would see to his punishment in this one as well.

The edict in which Theodosius imposed Nicene Catholicism as the state religion of the empire was issued at Thessalonica in 380, and it was emblematic of the new emperor's summary way of working and of his capacity for drastically simplifying problems. The Arians were the edict's primary targets, and in practice it condemned their church to death by slow strangulation.

With the pagans, Theodosius was at first a bit more cautious, but when he felt strong enough to do so, he took drastic measures against them, too. Sacrifices had long been forbidden, but in 391 the emperor definitively suppressed all pagan cults, closed their temples, and forbade under penalty of death any form of polytheistic worship; the following year, he extended the prohibition to the private worship of the Lares and Penates, the Roman household gods.

* * *

Unable to use so unilateral an approach in handling the crisis with the Goths, Theodosius showed himself capable of much greater flexibility. Obviously, the war was not over, and therefore his first goal was to reconstitute the army and resume operations against the Goths. The barbarians had to be made to understand that, despite their great victory at Adrianople, the Roman Empire was not yet defeated. Without losing any time, Theodosius promulgated some extremely harsh laws: Enlistment officials were required to sign up all conscripts at once, without allowing themselves to be swayed by exemptions or bribes; all proprietors of great estates had to furnish their quota of men, taking them from among the peasants who worked their land; all deserters, and all those who were obligated by law to perform military service but had so far, one way or another, managed to avoid it, had to report to their units or face a death sentence. The enlistment officials were authorized to draft, without any formalities, all soldiers' sons, all vagrants, all unemployed men without a permanent residence, and also all immigrants capable of bearing arms. The emperor threatened death by burning as the punishment for any administrator of a large estate who concealed the presence of an immigrant among his workers; all immigrants were to be reported and consigned to the enlistment officials.

With these drastic measures, Theodosius succeeded, for better or worse, in putting the army back on its feet; at the same time, he was hiring Hunnish and even Gothic mercenaries. Although the Goths had entered the empire in different groups and merged into a single army under Fritigern's command, they continued to be an aggregation of tribes, some of them with no connections at all to one another; many of those tribes had remained on the other side of the Danube, withdrawing to mountainous regions where they were able to keep the Huns at bay. Theodosius did not hesitate to open negotiations with their leaders, offering advantageous terms to any of them willing to furnish him with mercenaries to fight against the other Goths, and some of the leaders accepted the deal. One in particular, Athanaric, had once been very popular among the Goths, had fought against the Romans, and then had been more or less shoved aside, not least because he was old. Theodosius invited him to Constantinople, received him with all honors, and had his statue erected in the Hippodrome, next to those of Roman politicians; and although Athanaric died shortly afterward, many warriors had accompanied him to Constantinople, and they agreed to serve in the Roman army.

* * *

The army as rebuilt by Theodosius was not necessarily capable of succeeding where Valens's army had failed. The veterans who fell at Adrianople were not easy to replace, and the quality of the new units surely did not reach the level of those that had been destroyed. But Theodosius used the army not so much to defeat the Goths as to force them to negotiate and to accept a reasonable compromise. Even though Adrianople had been a crushing victory, the victors were still in a precarious situation. The Gothic leaders' strategic abilities were of little use if their men could not manage to take any cities; without fortified cities to serve as bases and winter quarters, the barbarians could be masters of Thrace, they could advance to the suburbs of Constantinople, but they could not say they had conquered the country. However well armed they might have been, they were still just vagabond marauders, and what was worse, the authority that Fritigern had won for himself in the moment of danger had partly dissolved the morning after the victory, when it seemed that anything was possible, and many chieftains had decided to strike out on their own.

Theodosius and Gratian conducted their operations prudently, reoccupying lost territory a little at a time, guaranteeing the security of Constantinople, and trying to show the Goths that the empire was still able to make them pay a heavy price. It was half a bluff, but in the end it was successful. One after another, the leaders of the various groups let themselves be persuaded to make peace, in exchange for the same concessions, more or less, that Valens had promised in the beginning and then taken back. Some of the leaders received cultivable land, enough for the families of their men to settle on, in the same territories they themselves had laid waste during years of pillage and atrocities; other chieftains received officers' appointments and stipends in the army, and their men were persuaded to enlist. At last, in 382, Theodosius scored a coup by convincing Fritigern, who was still in command of the largest Gothic band, that he should agree to talks.

The envoy sent to negotiate with Fritigern was Saturninus, who had directed operations against the Goths the year before Adrianople and was one of the generals who escaped the massacre by a whisker. Saturninus negotiated a treaty that at least in appearance satisfied everyone, and he was received in triumph upon returning to Constantinople. The following year, in recompense, the emperor appointed him consul.

The rhetorician Themistius, who a few years earlier had publicly congratulated Valens for making peace with the Goths, was charged with delivering an encomium in honor of Saturninus. In this oration, humanitarian rhetoric encountered before can be heard to vibrate anew, as if nothing had changed. Themistius lauded the government for having found a political solution to the problem, for receiving the Goths in peace instead of trying to annihilate them: "Philanthropy has prevailed over destruction. Would it perhaps have been better to fill Thrace with corpses instead of farmers? The barbarians are already transforming their weapons into hoes and sickles and cultivating the fields." This was the ideology of the "melting pot," viewing the barbarians as destined to be integrated into the empire as so many had been admitted in the past. Their descendants, Themistius said, "can't be called barbarians; for all intents and purposes, they're Romans. They pay the same taxes we do, they serve with us in the army, they're governed in the same way and subject to the same laws. And before long, the same thing will happen with the Goths."

In practice, Theodosius's solution to the Gothic problem had been in the air for a long time and more than once had been on the point of implementation before going awry. Valens had let the Goths into the empire with the idea of enlisting them in the army, and although the inefficiency and corruption that characterized the military authorities' treatment of the refugees had driven them to rebellion, Valens had always remained open to the prospect of a negotiated peace; indeed, just a few hours before being killed at Adrianople, the emperor had been involved in discussions with Fritigern's envoys, trying to find a solution. In 382, Theodosius did exactly what could have been done six years before, though he could not easily cancel out everything that had happened in the interval—the years of pillaging and atrocities, the destruction of an army, the death of an emperor, and the siege of the imperial capital. After Adrianople, enrolling Gothic warriors in the imperial army was much more difficult, as was explaining to the civilian population that the Goths were really just refugees, people who should receive humane treatment, a useful workforce.

And yet the ruling classes of the empire gave this a try, and one can either admire their goodwill or be astonished by their cynicism. To the politicians who collaborated with Theodosius, the acceptance of the Goths, despite everything that had happened, posed no problem at all; official speeches and the verses of the court poets all harped on the same string. A Gaulish rhetorician, Pacatus, enthused over all the new Roman soldiers, barbarians, yes, but so willing to learn: "O wonderful and memorable! Those who once had been enemies of Rome, now marching under Roman commanders and Roman banners, following the standards they used to fight against, filling as soldiers the cities they had formerly emptied and devastated as enemies. The Goth, the Hun, and the Alan, learning to express themselves according to the rules and taking their turn on guard duty and fearful of being criticized in their officers' reports." The tale of the barbarian who throws away his animal skins and learns to dress like a civilized person and obey orders and observe discipline was told again and again by the authors of Theodosius's time, and the implication was clear: Exchanging those bestial clothes for garb befitting a citizen and learning to live according to the rules made one a Roman. All the rhetoric about the universality of the empire, about its capacity for assimilation, was trotted out to demonstrate that Theodosius had made the right choice. And, to be clear, it wasn't all empty rhetoric; to a certain degree, that capacity for assimilation genuinely existed. The empire really was absorbing the barbarians, even though, as it did so, it inevitably changed.

* * *

The most striking example of how the Roman army absorbed and integrated the Goths is given by a group of gravestones found in the latter half of the nineteenth century in a paleochristian cemetery near Portogruaro, in the Veneto, where once stood a Roman city with a name of good augury, Concordia. A considerable number of these gravestones, almost forty, are dedicated to soldiers in Theodosius's army, soldiers from many different regiments—so many that people at first wondered why they had all been buried in this one particular place. Later research suggested that toward the end of his reign, in 394, Theodosius had fought a great battle more or less in that area against one of the usual usurpers, and part of his army probably remained encamped near Concordia for a long time, so we may conclude that the gravestones go back to that period. Since they come from a Christian cemetery, all the gravestones presumably memorialize soldiers who were Christians. Many regimental names are of the fanciful variety typical in the late empire—the Bracchiati, the Armigeri—and many have the names of barbarian tribes: The Heruli seniores, for example, or the Batavians, the unit held in reserve at the battle of Adrianople, whose troops had saved their skins by running away in time.

If you read the inscriptions on all these gravestones, they give the impression that the army was a very compact society, where everyone was linked to everyone else by ties of camaraderie or kinship, and also by religious bonds. In many cases, the inscription states that the dead man's gravestone has been paid for by his comrades-in-arms or by fellow villagers or countrymen serving in the same regiment; the frequent mention of wives demonstrates that the military was a real microcosm, in which men lived with their families. Moreover, the tone of these inscriptions is decorous and devout, and they offer many dedications and regards "to the best of colleagues," "to the holy church of the city of Concordia." But a close look at the names of the soldiers reveals that they were almost all barbarians. They all have Flavius as a first name, because it had been the name of the imperial family since the reign of Constantine, and every immigrant who was granted citizenship received that name; following Flavius, almost every soldier has a Germanic and in many cases even a Gothic name, such as Flavius Andila, a noncommissioned officer in the Bracchiati, or Flavius Sindila, who served in the Herulian regiment.

This was the positive face of integration, the proof that Theodosius's policy could succeed: The Goth became a Roman soldier, swore loyalty to the empire, learned to comply with military discipline and to appreciate his stipend and his pension; and the army, which was a community, seemed like the perfect machine for handling this integration process. It absorbed barbarians, ground them down, and transformed them into Roman veterans, into the men whom emperors in their public discourses addressed as "comrades in arms" and who constituted the real pillar of the empire.

XII

THE ANTIBARBARIAN REACTION

It would be wonderful if we could cite only the positive face of the medallion: if everything that remained to us of Theodosius's policy were the speeches by the rhetoricians who celebrated integration and the gravestones of the Gothic warriors transformed into stalwart Christian soldiers. But in reality, there was another face, and we must come to terms with that one, too.

The Goths were not always enlisted as soldiers in the regular army. In many cases, the agreements with their chieftains provided for hiring the soldiers as mercenaries, which meant that they remained members of autonomous bands and did not become Roman soldiers. The government consented to hire a barbarian band as a whole and quartered it somewhere in the empire, with the understanding that the provincials were obligated to maintain it. The mercenaries, that is, were billeted in people's houses and could requisition food, and if they became a little violent, the people just had to put up with them, because often the only Roman troops on the ground in a given place were those same barbarians, and nobody else could force them to behave.

In instances where Roman units and mercenary bands were quartered in the same area, the risk of incidents always existed: The soldiers were jealous of the barbarian mercenaries, who received better pay than they did, and at times Roman commanders themselves took steps to defend the population from thuggery, attacking the mercenaries and on occasion even slaughtering them. In such cases, the government intervened harshly in defense of the mercenaries, cashiering the culpable officers and remanding them for trial, because barbarians were to be treated well. The emperor was not strong enough to get rid of them and in fact actually needed them. After Adrianople, the conscription system stopped working, as the empire's citizens had no desire to be soldiers, and the barbarian mercenaries were such convenient replacements. Their units were already formed, battle-hardened, combat-ready, and with no need for training; it was enough to pay them and furnish them with the *annona*, the supplies of grain and other food they received from taxpayers who paid in kind. Theodosius could not have done without these foreign soldiers; during the course of his reign, he had to deal with two usurpers, both of them dangerous, and was able to overcome them only because his forces included, in addition to the regular army, barbarian mercenaries.

Before long, everyone realized that the barbarians had become indispensable, and the Christians saw in this state of affairs the confirmation of their belief that the world was approaching its end. St. Jerome denounced the emperors for having recourse to the warrior bands, comparing the Roman Empire to a colossus with feet made partly of iron and partly of clay: "Just as in the past, there was indeed nothing stronger and solider than the Roman empire, so now, at the end of time, there is nothing weaker, for whether we fight civil wars or foreign wars, we need the help of various barbarian peoples."

The emperors, on the other hand, tended to consider with satisfaction the new strength the mercenaries placed at their disposal. St. Ambrose related a conversation with Magnus Maximus, recently acclaimed as emperor by the army in Gaul, as he was preparing to do battle near Milan with one of Theodosius's generals, who was coming at the head of an army composed in large part of Gothic mercenaries. Ambrose reported that Magnus Maximus was almost offended: Look at this, he exclaimed, they're sending barbarians against me, "as if I don't have any to put on the battlefield myself, when I've got thousands and thousands of barbarians in my service. Every one of them gets the *annona* from me!" In short, if one wanted to seize power and hold it, one had to have barbarians on one's side. In certain regions of the empire, where the mercenaries had completely replaced the units of the regular army, the change was reflected in the language itself: In Syriac, starting at the end of the fourth century, the word for "soldier" became *Goth*.

* * *

Not surprisingly, a current of antibarbarian sentiment took shape among the governing circles of the empire in the last years of Theodosius's reign. Until that moment, everyone in any way connected to the government or educated in good schools seems to have been persuaded that the integration of the barbarians was both possible and desirable. At a certain point, however, a few people who disagreed began to appear. The most famous of them was an intellectual, Synesius, the proprietor of great estates in Africa who later became bishop of a city in Libya. Synesius experienced the years after Adrianople with growing rage; to him, the empire was terribly governed, and what exasperated him most was the excessive power of the barbarians. Not that Synesius was a racist; under certain conditions, he was not at all opposed to giving the barbarians work and trying to integrate them. When he spoke of his estates in Libya, under constant threat from Berber raids, he reserved his most contemptuous expressions for the soldiers who were supposed to protect the people: all cowards, Synesius said, and the officers all corrupt, thinking only of their payoffs. But by chance, a group of Hunnish mercenaries arrived in his vicinity, patrolled the desert, and let no Berber escape. Synesius was their enthusiastic admirer: though barbarians, when they were commanded by good officers they became true Romans. The Goths, however, were another matter, and Synesius felt the government was mad to turn the defense of the country over to them: "Only a madman wouldn't be afraid at seeing all these young men, who have grown up in foreign lands and still live according to their customs, charged with carrying out military activity in our country."

The explicit target of Synesius's invective was the recently dead Thedosius himself: The gist of his complaint was that Theodosius drew barbarians into the empire and gave them citizenship, land, and army commands even though they had Roman blood on their hands. The fact that career officers in command positions in the army—and even in the empire—were *Goths* was something that Synesius found particularly hard to swallow. Before Adrianople this practice had not frightened anyone; by the time Synesius was writing, however, opinions had shifted, and many people had come to consider such openness dangerous. Synesius drew a famous portrait of the immigrants, still thoroughly rough and unpolished, who nonetheless acted like the masters of the empire. A Christian intellectual, but one imbued with pagan philosophical culture and all the haughtiness of a great landowner from a senatorial family, Synesius was outraged by the kind of spectacle that could be seen every day, "when one dressed in animal skins gives commands to others wearing the chlamys, and when a man takes off the fur coat that covered him, dons the toga, and joins the Roman magistrates to discuss the items on the agenda with the consul, who offers him the seat of honor next to himself, while those who should have the right to it stand back. And then, as soon as such a man as this leaves the Senate chambers, he immediately puts on his furry clothes again, and when he meets his fellows, they all laugh about the toga. If you've got one of those things on, they say, you can't draw your sword."

* * *

After the death of Theodosius in 395, opposing views on his politics of compromise, which included receiving the Goths into the empire, were expressed with increasing violence. Many continued to exalt the capacity of the universal empire to open itself genuinely to all mankind, and they wanted the emperor to present himself as a father not only to the Romans but to all the peoples of the world. Conversely, others argued that to let so many immigrants enter the empire at the same time, not to mention enlisting them in that most delicate of governmental sectors, national defense, was dangerous. Undoubtedly a weak point in Theodosius's policy was the fact that the army of the East had been crippled by the losses at Adrianople and therefore obliged to rebuild itself in haste and at any cost. The cost, in fact, was high: To have an efficient military force at his disposal, the emperor could not do without his Goths, and for many people this was a sign of intolerable weakness that presaged no good for the Roman state.

In the last years of his life, Theodosius had become sole emperor of the Roman Empire. Upon his death, the empire had been divided between his two sons, Arcadius in the East and Honorius in the West, but one was a teenager and the other a child. They were both weak rulers, in thrall to their eunuchs and their barbarian generals, and certain subjects that could not be broached under Theodosius were frankly discussed under his sons. Synesius addressed the elder, Arcadius, in no uncertain terms: Your father, he said, was responsible for ruining the empire; he could have brought the Goths to their knees, but instead he lifted them up and gave them so much room that now we're all in their hands.

Historians have spoken of an antibarbarian reaction and have even posited a political party that included senators and intellectuals who felt the same way Synesius did. The reality was perhaps not so simple: The politics of the imperial court was intricate, deceit and treachery were rife, and to protest against the barbarians and call for a return to the good old days when certain things didn't happen could have been a useful gambit in the struggle for power. Most people ultimately shared the assumptions about the empire's ability to assimilate the barbarians but resisted granting them too much power too quickly and thereby abdicating the civilizing mission of the empire. In the end, certain speeches in the Senate, certain discourses delivered in the presence of the emperor, served chiefly to ruin the politicians and generals of the adverse party and to raise up other politicians and generals who might have been of barbarian origin as well. A great number of Gothic generals emerged in the years of Theodosius's reign and afterward in the reigns of his two sons. Before this, the barbarians who made careers for themselves in the imperial army had come, for the most part, from the lands across the Rhine, from the Franks and the Alamanni. Under Theodosius and his sons, the Goths started reaching the top ranks, too, and this created competition and altered the power balance among the cliques and lobbies that vied for influence at court.

* * *

The ascension of barbarian generals under Theodosius and his successors was only the natural outcome of a process of immigrant absorption that had been under way in the empire for a long time; the disaster at Adrianople and Theodosius's subsequent accords with the Goths had accelerated this process, had made it more conspicuous, and led to the speedy Romanizing, or Hellenizing, of the leaders involved. This certainly must have been the case with Fritigern, who already had all the qualities necessary to become an outstanding Roman general, although nothing more was heard of him after the treaty he concluded with Theodosius. In the years around 400, another general who was the son of Gothic immigrants, Fravitta, played an important role in the politics of Constantinople, and contemporary sources reveal that he was "a barbarian by birth, but for all the rest a Greek, not only in his habits, but also in his character and his religion."

Another general of Gothic origin was Alaric. Born outside the empire but resident inside it from the days of his youth, he became a Roman citizen and was surely as much at ease in a toga as he was in the animal skins of his tribe. In the year 410, he was the commander of the Goths who sacked Rome. Yet he was a career soldier who started among the Gothic mercenaries in Theodosius's service. He rapidly became a commander, which means that he had a band of warriors who followed him because he knew how to negotiate lucrative contracts with the government.

Alaric's career is emblematic of the empire's weakness in the first years after Adrianople, at least in the East, where mercenaries had become an indispensable buttress of imperial authority. When all was said and done, their loyalty depended on one thing only: Whether they were well paid. When the government had money and paid them, Alaric and other such military leaders fought for the emperor, rendering precious service, helping to defend the frontiers, quash usurpations, and put down rebellions, even if occasionally the rebels were other Gothic mercenaries like themselves. The commanders were civilized enough to understand how things worked in the empire: One had to play politics, intrigue in corridors, find supporters, and when things went wrong, one had to be capable of thoroughly unscrupulous blackmail in order to move forward. Alaric negotiated various agreements with the government, asking for more every time: stipends, pensions, wealth to distribute to his men, and land, because the dream of every mercenary was to have his house and his slaves, and to live a tranquil life on his own property.

For himself, and in addition to money, Alaric asked for ranks, titles, a political position; and when the government seemed reluctant to fulfill his requests, Alaric, like many other commanders, had no scruples about rebelling and threatened to sack the country instead of defending it. At times, the government stood firm and sent other generals, other barbarian mercenaries, against him; more than once, Alaric pushed too hard, more than once he found himself trapped with his people in situations from which there seemed to be no way out, but he always managed to get a last-minute reprieve, to sign a truce, to resume negotiations. This period was a tragedy for the parts of the countryside such bands moved through, just as the pre-Adrianople years of Gothic devastation in Thrace had been a tragedy, but sometimes one gets the impression that for the generals this was only a way of conducting politics, and that in the end they were always ready to come to terms among themselves.

Alaric finally acceded to command of all the Roman troops in Illyricum. He was the probable object of Synesius's disdain when the orator described the barbarian taking off his animal skins and putting on a toga to enter the Senate chamber and discuss matters with the magistrates, but then changing back to his skins as soon as he could, because the toga made him uncomfortable. A man with at least two identities, he was Alaric, the warrior chieftain to whom so many Goths had sworn loyalty according to the rituals of their ancestors, and Flavius Alaricus, the Roman general, the *magister militum*.

* * *

The question remains: Is 378 really a date of epochal importance, the end of antiquity and the beginning of the Middle Ages?

Often when one looks more closely, boundaries become less clear, breaks seem less drastic; one often discovers that the great changes actually had begun earlier and that the past, for its part, took a good long while to die. Nonetheless, the battle of Adrianople marks an abrupt, dramatic acceleration in the process by which the Roman Empire opened its borders to barbarian immigration, a process that had already been going on for some time and transforming the society, the army, and the very government of the empire.

The importance of geography in these events proved decisive. The entire series of events herein described transpired in the Eastern Roman Empire; the Goths presented themselves on the eastern border in the autumn of 376; the eastern emperor admitted them and then quickly regretted what he had done; the battle of Adrianople was fought in a region that today is part of Turkey; Theodosius reigned in the East; his army re-formed itself after the battle by absorbing Gothic volunteers and engaging Gothic mercenaries.

Thus, also in the East, people began, after a while, to understand the destabilizing consequences of these choices: There intolerance toward barbarians sprang up and spread; there violent incidents between the civilian population and the Goths broke out; there most of the mercenary units were stationed and the principal Gothic commanders, among them Alaric, made their military careers. After a while, the East decided it had had enough of the barbarian problem and wished to be free of it forever. When the mercenaries became too turbulent, when their commanders put forth a few too many demands, the government of the East began working to transfer them a little farther west, making them promises and granting them concessions, provided that every time the barbarians took a few more steps westward. In the years of Arcadius and Honorius, the West was governed badly, its energies consumed in the struggle to keep the barbarians across the Rhine at bay, and eventually it succumbed to this eastern policy. By dint of treaties and settlements that were always provisional and always subject to further debate, the bulk of the barbarian mercenaries—under Alaric, who by this time had become their supreme commander—moved into Italy. There, for a while, the western government managed to pay them and keep them happy;

when it could no longer do so, in 410 the Roman general Alaric, wishing to show that he was serious, marched on Rome and sacked it.

From this time on, the flood of barbarian immigrants, which grew more and more violent and over which the weak western governments ceased to exercise any sort of control, began moving steadily westward. When the barbarian mercenaries finally seized power, it was in the West—the Goths in southern Gaul and in Spain, the Franks in northern Gaul—so that at length the Western Roman Empire dissolved, while the empire of the East continued to exist.

And this really was an epochal turning point, because it marked the end of the ancient unity of the Roman and Mediterranean world. It also marked the birth of a new West, where Romans and Germans would have to learn, laboriously, to live together, and of a Greek East, whose history would be completely different. The consequences of that split can still be felt in Europe today.

SUGGESTIONS FOR FURTHER READING

The following pages contain some suggestions for readers interested in further study of the subjects considered in this book. The international bibliography on these matters is huge, but I've tried to include at least the most significant works. In addition, specialists or anyone else who wishes to check the sources used herein will find them referenced by chapter number.

A great part of the account of the battle of Adrianople and the events that preceded it is based on a single, crucial source: the fourth-century historian Ammianus Marcellinus (hereinafter AM). Greek by origin, a native of Antioch, and a career officer in the military in the years 350–60, Ammianus wrote his *History* in Latin toward the end of the century. There are English translations by John C. Rolfe in the Loeb Classical Library (in 3 volumes; Cambridge, Mass., 1939; often reprinted) and by Walter Hamilton in a Penguin Classics volume titled *Ammianus Marcellinus: The Later Roman Empire* (London, 1986; reprinted 2004).

The other important contemporary treatment, only fragments of which have come down to us, was written in Greek by Eunapius of Sardis, who was born in 349 and who, like Ammianus, wrote his history at the end of the fourth century. What survives of Eunapius's work is available in English translation in R. C. Blockley, *The Fragmentary Classicising Historians of the Later Roman Empire*, 2 vols. (Liverpool, 1981–1983).

For a basic introduction to the period, see Averil Cameron, *The Later Roman Empire: AD 284–430* (Cambridge, Mass., 1993); Peter Brown, *The Making of Late Antiquity* (Cambridge, Mass., 1978; reprinted 1993);

and Hartwin Brandt, *Das Ende der Antike. Geschichte des spätrömischen Reiches* (Munich, 2001). For in-depth study, the following collective works in Italian are fundamental: *Società romana e impero tardoantico*, ed. Andrea Giardina, 4 vols. (Roma-Bari, 1986), and *Storia di Roma*, 4 vols. in seven books (Torino, 1988–1993), vol. 3, *L'età tardoantica*, in two books, ed. A. Carandini, L. Cracco Ruggini, and A. Giardina (Torino, 1993).

The international bibliography on the subject of the Goths is vast. Works available in English include: E. A. Thompson, *The Visigoths in the Time of Ulfila* (Oxford, 1966); Herwig Wolfram, *History of the Goths*, trans. Thomas J. Dunlop (Los Angeles, 1988); P. J. Heather, *Goths and Romans, 332–489* (Oxford, 1991); P. J. Heather and J. F. Matthews, *The Goths in the Fourth Century* (Liverpool, 1991); and P. J. Heather, *The Goths* (Oxford-Cambridge, 1996).

Modern reconstructions of the conflict between the empire and the Goths abound. In Italian, see principally the works of Maria Cesa: *376–382:* "Romani e barbari sul Danubio," in *Studi Urbinati* 57 (1984), pp. 63–99, and *Impero tardoantico e barbari. La crisi militare da Adrianopoli al 418* (Como, 1994). In addition, there is the volume *Romani e Barbari. Incontro e scontro di culture*, ed. S. Giorcelli Bersani (Torino, 2004).

The following pages contain more specific references to aspects of the campaign and the battle of Adrianople as treated in the present work, arranged according to the individual chapters.

PROLOGUE

1 On the deposition of Romulus Augustulus, see A. Momigliano, "La caduta senza rumore di un Impero nel 476 d.C.," in *Concetto, storia, miti e immagini del Medio Evo*, ed. V. Branca (Firenze, 1973), pp. 409–28.

2 **the Roman province of Thrace:** Technically speaking, Thrace was actually much more than a province; it was one of the twelve dioceses into which Diocletian had divided the empire and was itself subdivided into six provinces, one of which was also called Thrace.

I. THE ROMAN EMPIRE IN THE FOURTH CENTURY

3 A vast, recent, and innovative bibliography exists on the subject of the Roman frontiers. For an introduction to the topic, see the overview provided by C. R. Whittaker, "Le frontiere imperiali," in *Storia di Roma*, ed. A. Carandini, L. Cracco Ruggini, and A. Giardina, vol. 3, *L'età tardoantica*, book 1, *Crisi e trasformazione* (Torino, 1993), pp. 369–423.

4 **crisscrossed by cargo ships:** In the fourth century, Mediterranean commerce was already in an obvious downward phase, but some routes prospered, particularly the ones over which African products were brought to Italy. See C. Panella, "Merci e scambi nel Mediterraneo tardoantico," in *Storia di Roma*, vol. 3, book 2, *I luoghi e le culture*, pp. 613–97. Also of interest are the stimulating observations of C. Wickham, "Marx, Sherlock Holmes and Late Roman Commerce," in Wickham, *Land and Power: Studies in Italian and European Social History, 400–1200* (London, 1994), pp. 77–98.

4 **a metropolis of one million inhabitants:** The population of Rome in the fourth century has in fact been calculated in various ways. See R. Krautheimer, *Rome: Profile of a City, 312–1308* (Princeton, 1980), p. 4, where the population is estimated at eight hundred thousand inhabitants.

5 Edward Gibbon's magnum opus, *The History of the Decline and Fall of the Roman Empire*, is available in various editions, including the three-volume Penguin edition by D. Womersley (London, 1994).

5 On the great transformation of the empire during and after the crisis of the third century, the most recent and suggestive study is J.-M. Carrié and A. Rousselle, *L'Empire romain en mutation des Sévères à Constantin, 192–337* (Paris, 1999).

8 **Catholic Christianity:** Theodosius defines as "Christian Catholics" those who follow the doctrine approved by the Council of Nicaea, according to which "we should believe in the unique deity of the Father, the Son, and the Holy Spirit, of equal majesty, and in the Holy Trinity" (*Codex Theodosianus*, 16.1.2). Another formulation, this one from the following year, declares that Christians are those who "acknowledge that the Father, the Son, and the Holy Spirit are of single majesty and power, with the same glory and a single splendor," which confession is equivalent to "the true Nicene faith" (ibid., 16.1.1). These decrees principally targeted the Arians, who believed in a Christ inferior to the Father, created and not eternal. Please note that the qualification *catholic* here does not yet imply the recognition of a Roman papacy and is for all practical purposes synonymous with *orthodox*.

II. THE EMPIRE AND THE BARBARIANS

10 **to pose as masters of the world:** See Claude Nicolet, *Space, Geography, and Politics in the Early Roman Empire*, trans. Hélene

Leclerc (Ann Arbor, 1991). The original French title is *L'Inventaire du monde: Géographie et politiques aux origines de l'Empire romain* (Paris, 1988).

10 The reader interested in studying the conflict between Rome and Persia may begin with the ample collection of documents and commentary in M. H. Dodgeon and S. N. C. Lieu, *The Roman Eastern Frontier and the Persian Wars, AD 226–363: A Documentary History* (London, 1991).

10 On Rome's relationships with Arab and African nomads, there exists an extremely rich bibliography. Basic studies include I. Shahîd, *Rome and the Arabs* (Cambridge, MA, 1984); the same author's *Byzantium and the Arabs in the Fourth Century* (Cambridge, MA, 1984); and Y. Modéran, *Les Maures et l'Afrique romaine, IVe-VIIe siècle* (Rome, 2003).

11 **Some zealous Christians were bothered:** St. Augustine, *Letters*, 46–47.

11 **Roman writers rejoiced:** Selection of texts in F. Borca, *Confrontarsi con l'altro: I romani e la Germania* (Milan, 2004), pp. 23–26.

13 On the Romans' attitude toward barbarians, see Y.-A. Dauge, *Le Barbare: Recherches sur la conception romaine de la barbarie et de la civilisation* (Bruxelles, 1981); for the specific period under consideration here, see G. B. Ladner, "On Roman Attitudes towards Barbarians in Late Antiquity," in *Viator* 7 (1976), pp. 1–26, and A. Chauvot, *Opinions romaines face aux barbares au IVe siècle après J.-C.* (Paris, 1998).

13 **the government was obliged to evacuate the inhabitants of the most exposed areas:** The most significant of these operations was the Roman withdrawal from Dacia, the province on the far side of the Danube which Trajan had conquered and Aurelian decided to abandon a century and a half later. On the debate concerning the actual effectiveness of the evacuation of the Roman population, see L. Okamura, "Roman Withdrawals from Three Transfluvial Frontiers," in *Shifting Frontiers in Late Antiquity*, ed. R. W. Mathisen and H. S. Sivan (Aldershot, 1996), pp. 11–19.

13 **threatened to arm their farmworkers:** Synesius, *Epistola*, 125.

14 **to work on his land for free:** *Panegyrici Latini*, 8.9; *Codex Theodosianus*, 5.6.3.

14 **obligated to furnish the army with recruits:** There is a clear description of the system in S. Mazzarino, *Aspetti sociali del IV secolo* (Rome, 1951), pp. 249ff.

15 **The barbarians were a potential resource:** Themistius, 10; AM, 9.11, 31.4.

15 **Governmental departments arose:** These government officials were the *praefecti laetorum*, whose nature has not always been correctly interpreted by historians. See, nevertheless, E. Demougeot, "À propos des lètes gaulois du IVe siècle," in *Beiträge zur alten Geschichte und deren Nachleben: Festschrift für Franz Altheim* (Berlin, 1969–70), vol. 2, pp. 101–13, and C. J. Simpson, "*Laeti* in the *Notitia Dignitatum*: 'Regular' Soldiers versus 'Soldier-Farmers,'" *Revue Belge de Philologie et d'Histoire* 66 (1988), pp. 80–85.

III. THE GOTHS AND ROME

17 **they were lacking the knowledge of comparative linguistics:** See, however, H. Wolfram, *History of the Goths*, trans. Thomas J. Dunlop (Los Angeles, 1988), p. 397 (note 58 to p. 44): "the philologist Jerome must have known that the Goths spoke a Germanic language."

18 **being tall and blond was a mark of inferiority:** See, for example, the famous passage in Eunapius, fragment 37, on the effect that the sight of the Gothic prisoners had on the inhabitants of the Roman cities, who had never seen them before: "They aroused the contempt of those who saw their bodies, uselessly tall, too heavy for their feet, and narrow through the middle, as Aristotle says of insects."

18 **only their original nucleus was formed by small, almond-eyed people with Mongolian features:** "According to current research, Mongolian types made up 20–25% of the Huns" (I. Bóna, *Les Huns: Le grand empire barbare d'Europe, IVe–Ve siècles* [Paris, 2002], p. 25).

18 **the Visigoths and the Ostrogoths:** For the origin of this nomenclature, see Wolfram, *History of the Goths*, pp. 19–26 ("the idea that the Visigoths are the western Goths and the Ostrogoths the eastern Goths is no older than Cassiodorus's entrance into the service of Theoderic the Great").

21 **Since the majority of those mercenaries would wind up being killed:** Libanius, 59.93. Other references to the use of Gothic mercenaries against the Persians can be found in Libanius, 12.62,

12.78, 18.169, and in AM, 20.8.1, 23.2.7, 30.2.6, 31.6.1, 31.16.8.

22 **the Gothic people venerated his memory and his name:** Eutropius, 10.7; Jordanes, *Getica,* 21.

22 **"treated our emperor as if he were theirs":** Libanius, 59.89–90.

22 **regular shipments of grain, carried across the Danube:** Themistius, 10.10, and Julian (the Apostate), *The Caesars*, 329A.

22 **probably would not have been able to survive:** See AM, 27.5.7. The theory that the very presence of the empire and the trade it generated was a factor in the barbarians' dependence and ultimately in the destabilization of the barbarian populations outside the empire has been convincingly sustained by C. R. Whittaker, "Trade and Frontiers in the Roman Empire," in *Trade and Famine in Classical Antiquity,* ed. P. Garnsey and C. R. Whittaker (Cambridge, 1983), pp. 110–27. See also C. R. Whittaker, "Supplying the System: Frontiers and Beyond," in *Barbarians and Romans in North-West Europe,* ed. J. C. Barrett, A. P. Fitzpatrick, and L. Macinnes (Oxford, 1989), pp. 64–79.

23 **"the radiant stone on the bank of the Dnieper":** I have taken this quotation from the Italian translation of H. Wolfram's *History of the Goths*, whose English translation is otherwise cited in these notes. The quotation in question ("*la pietra radiosa sulla spiaggia del Dnepr*") is found only in the Italian edition of the text, which was "revised and expanded by the author." See H. Wolfram, *Storia dei Goti* (Rome, 1985), p. 57.

23 The chronology of Ulfila's life and of the Christianization of the Goths is a topic of some controversy. See E. A. Thompson, *The Visigoths in the Time of Ulfila* (Oxford, 1966), pp. xiii–xxiii, and H. Wolfram, *History of the Goths*, pp. 75–85.

25 The "Passions" of the Gothic martyrs, the most famous among whom is St. Sabas the Goth, are published in H. Delehaye, "Saints de Thrace et de Mésie," *Analecta Bollandiana* 31 (1912), pp. 161–300.

26 For a study of Valens and his reign, see N. Lenski, *Failure of Empire: Valens and the Roman State in the Fourth Century A.D.* (Berkeley, 2002). The portrait and assessment of Valens are in AM, 31.14.

27 For Valens's religious policies, the principal (and hostile) source is Sozomen's *Historia Ecclesiastica*, 6.6–21, 39–40.

28 On Valens's first campaigns against the Goths, aside from the works already cited, see T. S. Burns, *Barbarians within the Gates of Rome: A Study of Roman Military Policy and the Barbarians, ca. 375–425 A.D.* (Bloomington, 1994).

30 The texts quoted in this paragraph are Themistius, 10; *Panegyrici Latini*, 11.16 ("the opportunity to be Roman"); *Codex Theodosianus*, 13.11.10, for the year 399 ("following the dream of Roman felicity"). Themistius's discourse has been much studied; a recent analysis in Italian is U. Roberto, "Temistio sulla politica gotica dell'imperatore Valente," *Annali dell'Istituto Italiano per gli Studi Storici* 14 (1997), pp. 137–203. For a broader contextualization, see P. J. Heather and D. Moncur, *Politics, Philosophy, and*

Empire in the Fourth Century: Select Orations of Themistius (Liverpool, 2001).

30 **he began to enlist Gothic troops:** I believe that some controversial passages in AM, in particular 30.2.6, 31.6.1, and 31.16.8, should be interpreted in this sense.

31 **a great wave of Gothic slaves** and **"Any family that is even moderately well-off":** Synesius, *De regno*, 15; Themistius, 10.11; Eunapius, fragment 42; AM, 31.6.5. It is probable that this situation is—anachronistically—reflected in a passage in the *Historia Augusta, Claud. 9* ("The Life of Claudius," that is, the Emperor Claudius II Gothicus, who reigned from 268 to 270): "the Roman provinces filled with barbarian slaves and Scythian husbandmen. The Goth was made the tiller of the barbarian frontier, nor was there a single district which did not have Gothic slaves in triumphant servitude."

IV. THE EMERGENCY OF 376

30 The principal contemporary account of the events that took place between 376 and 378 is contained in book 31 of Ammianus Marcellinus's *History*. This should be supplemented by the surviving fragments (30–44) of Eunapius's book 6.

34 **to the imperial library in search of further information:** Ammianus Marcellinus, at least, went there to have a look and concluded that the Hunnish people were "little known to ancient historians" (31.2.1). Eunapius, who was writing a little later, asserted that he found "in the Ancients" some material on the

Huns, but it was obviously written "when no one had anything precise to say" about that people (fragment 41).

35 The Roman image of the Huns in this period is conveyed to us in AM, 31.2. A popularizing treatment of the Huns can be found in H. Schreiber, *Die Hunnen: Attila probt den Weltuntergang* (Düsseldorf, 1976). An exhaustive though unfinished study in English is O. J. Maenchen-Helfen (ed. Max Knight), *The World of the Huns: Studies in their History and Culture* (Berkeley, 1973). In Italian, important scientific contributions are collected in the volume *Popoli delle steppe: Unni, Avari, Ungari*, Spoleto 1989 (35th Settimana del Centro Italiano di Studi sull'Alto Medioevo). For a more recent scientific treatment, see Bóna, *Les Huns*; this author definitively distances himself from the prejudices of Ammianus Marcellinus, "who, in the calm of his Roman office, had (fortunately for him) never met a Hun" (p. 5).

36 **excellently fashioned iron arrowheads:** Bóna, *Les Huns*, p. 24.

36 **almost as a genocide:** Eunapius, fragment 42.

36 **a legend . . . soon began to spread among them:** Jordanes, *Getica*, 24.

38 Historians have copiously discussed the problem of depopulation and the need for manpower in the Roman Empire. The discussion was opened by A. E. R. Boak, *Manpower Shortage and the Fall of the Roman Empire* (Ann Arbor/London, 1955); on the exact significance of the said depopulation, see in particular C. R. Whittaker, "*Agri Deserti*," in *Studies in Roman Property*,

ed. M. I. Finley (Cambridge, 1976), pp. 137–175, and the same author's "Labour Supply in the Late Roman Empire," *Opus* 1 (1982), pp.171–79. Recent reflections on immigration as a response to the need for manpower are presented in G. Wirth, "Rome and Its Germanic Partners in the Fourth Century," in *Kingdoms of the Empire: The Integration of Barbarians in Late Antiquity*, ed. W. Pohl (Leiden/New York/Köln, 1997), pp.13–55, and in C. R. Whittaker, "The Use and Abuse of Immigrants in the Later Roman Empire," in his essay collection *Rome and Its Frontiers: The Dynamics of Empire* (London/New York, 2004), pp. 199–218.

39 The origin and nature of the Roman colonate, the system of private land-tenancy by *coloni* (tenant farmers), is one of the most-discussed topics in recent historiography. See E. Lo Cascio, ed., *Terre, proprietari e contadini dell'impero romano. Dall'affitto agrario al colonato tardoantico* (Rome, 1997).

40 **humanitarian assistance . . . and then, down the road, the prospect of housing and work:** AM, 31.4.8 ("the emperor ordered that they should be given food for their present needs and fields to cultivate").

40 The stone bridge Constantine had contructed at Oescus-Sucidava, in the province of Dacia Ripensis, was almost one and a half miles long, but apparently it was no longer usable in Valens's day. The other bridges mentioned in fourth-century sources, particularly in reference to Valens's previous campaigns against the Goths, were only pontoon bridges of a provisional nature. See Wolfram, *History of the Goths*, pp. 65–67, and Whittaker, "Le frontiere imperiali," p. 408 (see chap. I, first note).

43 **allowing the military to address the problem in its own characteristic fashion:** "Those who governed with the emperor and exercised great power derided their bellicosity and said that they didn't know how to reason like politicians" (Eunapius, fragment 42).

44 **for the humanitarian assistance they hoped to receive:** AM, 31.4.12 ("ut simili susciperetur humanitate").

45 **Corruption was endemic in the Roman Empire:** See R. MacMullen, *Corruption and the Decline of Rome* (New Haven, 1988).

46 **The barbarians numbered tens of thousands:** Naturally, no precise estimate is possible; the figure of "almost 200,000" given by Eunapius (fragment 42) should be understood as employed for rhetorical effect.

V. THE OUTBREAK OF WAR

The history of the military campaigns that concluded with the battle of Adrianople has been reconstructed many times; however, such reconstructions have always been based on the same scanty sources we are familiar with. The most detailed reconstruction of the campaigns, including chronological and topological considerations, is in U. Wanke, *Die Gotenkriege des Valens: Studien zu Topographie und Chronologie im unteren Donauraum von 366 bis 378 n. Chr.* (Frankfurt am Main/New York, 1990). Very useful, even though chiefly addressed to nonspecialist readers, is S. MacDowall, *Adrianople, AD 378: The Goths Crush Rome's Legions* (Botley, 2001). (This is number 84 in Osprey

Publishing's popular *Campaign* series, well known to enthusiasts of military history and uniformology.)

51 Only hypotheses are possible when estimating the number of troops available to Lupicinus and Fritigern; here I follow MacDowall, *Adrianople, AD 378*, pp. 42ff. These estimates are partially based on an analysis of the troops normally stationed in Thrace.

The principal studies in Italian on the evolution of the Roman army in late antiquity are those of J.-M. Carrié, "L'esercito, trasformazioni funzionali ed economie locali," in *Societá romana e impero tardoantico*, ed. A. Giardina (Rome/Bari, 1986), vol. 1, *Istituzioni ceti, economie*, pp. 449–88, and "Eserciti e strategie," in *Storia di Roma*, vol. 3, book 1, pp. 83–154.

52 On the troops' equipment, see H. Elton, *Warfare in Roman Europe, AD 350–425* (Oxford, 1996), pp. 107–17. On their way of fighting, which the use of the spear had rendered more similar to the tactics of the ancient hoplitic phalanx, see M. J. Nicasie, *Twilight of Empire: The Roman Army from the Reign of Diocletian until the Battle of Adrianople* (Amsterdam, 1988), pp. 187–219, and P. Richardot, *La fin de l'armée romaine, 284–476* (Paris, 2001), pp. 253–69.

On the general poverty of the barbarians and the scantiness of their ornament, see Elton, *Warfare in Roman Europe*, pp. 15–88.

55 **Two Gothic chieftains . . . who had been in Valens's service for years:** The view of Sueridus and Colias—"*Gothorum optimates*," AM, 31.6—as mercenary commanders hired by Valens for the war against Persia is nothing like universally accepted, but I consider it far and away the most economical in comparison with other views, which postulate a prior reception and settlement of immigrant *dediticii* or *foederati*.

VI. THE BATTLE BY THE WILLOWS

The account of the battle is based entirely upon AM, 31.7.

62 A very large bibliography exists on the subject of the Romanized barbarian generals. To cite a few: D. Hoffmann, "Waldomar, Bacurius und Hariulf. Zur Laufbahn adliger und fürstlicher Barbaren im spätrömischen Heere des 4. Jahrhunderts," *Museum Helveticum* 35 (1981), pp. 307–18; H. Castritus, "Zur Sozialgeschichte der Heermeister des Westreichs," *Mitt. Inst. Österr. Geschichtsforschung* 92 (1984), pp. 1–33; A. Chauvot, "Origine sociale et carrière des barbares impériaux au IVe siècle," in *La mobilité sociale dans le monde romain*, ed. E. Frézouls (Strasbourg, 1992), pp. 173–84; and L. Cracco Ruggini, "Les généraux francs aux IVe et Ve siècles et leurs groupes aristocratiques," in *Clovis, Histoire et Mémoire*, ed. M. Rouche (Paris, 1997), pp. 673–88.

63 The quotation from Ammianus Marcellinus can be found in 31.7.8; on the state of mind in the Roman camp, see AM, 31.7.9.

64 **According to their custom, the barbarians renewed the oath to their commanders . . . and brothers in arms made the same pledge to one another:** I acknowledge that this is an extrapolation from Ammianus Marcellinus's much briefer phrase ("barbari postquam inter eos ex more iuratum est," AM 31.7.10), but this interpretation seems to me defensible in the light of what we know about the importance that a chieftain's followers had among the Visigoths, during the period in question and also later (Thompson, *The Visigoths*, pp. 51–53), and, more generally, about the importance of warriors' loyalty among the Germanic peoples.

65 For Totila, see Procopius of Caesarea, *De bello Gothico*, 4.31. Attention has been called to this episode by F. Cardini, *Alle radici della cavalleria medievale* (Florence, 1981), p. 29; the volume opens with a memorable evocation of the battle of Adrianople (pp. 3–6).

66 **Several thousand men were on each side:** A certain count is impossible; see the attempts made by P. Richardot, *La Fin de l'armée romaine, 284–476* (Paris, 2001), p. 273, and by MacDowall, *Adrianople, AD 378*, pp. 51ff. (I do not believe, however, as the latter author does, that the Goths who fought in the battle by the Willows represented only a separate band and not the bulk of Fritigern's force.)

68 The paragraph on the funeral rites for the fallen Goths is entirely inductive, based on what we know of the burial customs of the Germans and of the peoples of the steppe; Ammanius Marcellinus limits himself to informing us that the Goths voluntarily remained closed inside their wagon-circle for seven days. The inductions made, however, are not arbitrary. The theory that the Goths were still practicing human sacrifice throughout the fourth century is in Thompson, *The Visigoths*, p. 60 and note; in all probability, sacrifices of this kind accompanied the burial of Alaric as well (Jordanes, *Getica*, 30; and see Thompson, *The Visigoths*, p. 92). Sacrifices, and more specifically sacrifices of female slaves and concubines at the burials of pagan Germanic tribal leaders, are described by Arab travelers of the tenth century, among them the celebrated Ibn Fadhlan: see J. Brondsted,

The Vikings (Penguin, 1960; new translation 1965), pp. 252–491. For the funeral songs, see the fifth- and sixth-century sources assembled in Thompson, *The Visigoths*, p. 92. For the sacrifice of the dead man's horses, see the suggestions in Cardini, *Alle radici della cavalleria medievale*, pp. 31–52.

VII. THE WAR GOES ON

72 **a region that the Romans had attempted to populate long before:** The populating of the Dobrogea (or Dobruja) region, the territory between the Lower Danube River and the Black Sea, an area which included the Danube delta, had been effected both by the transfer of *coloni* and Roman veterans and by the deportation of a people, the Bessi, from the Balkan interior. See E. Condurachi, "Tiberio Plauzio Eliano e il trasferimento del 100.000 Transdanubiani nella Mesia," *Epigrqphica* 19 (1957), pp. 49–65, and A. G. Poulter, "Rural Communities (*vici* and *komai*) and Their Role in the Organisation of the Lines of Moesia Inferior," in *Roman Frontier Studies 1979: Papers presented to the 12th International Congress of Roman Frontier Studies*, ed. W. S. Hanson and L. J. F. Keppie (Oxford, 1980), pp. 729–44.

75 **impossible to travel through because they lacked human inhabitants:** Eunapius, fragment 42.

75 **the Thracian refugees got as far as Italy:** Ambrose mentions this in a letter of 379 to the bishop of Cesena (*Epistles*, 2, 28); see L. Cracco Ruggini, "Uomini senza terra e terra senza uomini nell'Italia antica," *Quaderni di sociologia rurale* 3 (1962), p. 33.

75 On the clash at Dibaltum, see AM, 31.8.9–10.

76 On the Cornuti, see the famous article by A. Alföldy, "Cornuti: A Teutonic Contingent in the Service of Constantine the Great and Its Decisive Role in the Battle at the Milvian Bridge," *Dumbarton Oaks Papers* 13 (1959), pp. 169–79.

77 **"more refined food than usual":** AM, 31.9.1.

78 On the Taifali, see AM, 31.9.5.

80 **"might have slaughtered the lot of them":** AM, 31.9.4.

VIII. VALENS MOVES

83 For the events narrated in this section, see AM, 31.10 and Eunapius, fragment 42.

85 **Valens was hooted:** Sozomen, 6.39; AM, 31.11.1.

87 **reduced everything to a question of culture:** Eunapius, fragment 44.1.

87 On Sebastianus, Eunapius (fragment 44.3–4) provides more ample information than Ammianus (AM, 31.11.2).

89 **two large, permanent encampments:** "Praesidiis fixis" (AM, 31.11.2).

90 **Sebastianus probably conducted his harassing operations successfully for some time:** The paragraph on Sebastianus's successes isn't a merely inductive reconstruction but is rather

based on Fritigern's reactions to Sebastianus's operations (AM, 31.11.5) and on Ammianus's reference (AM, 31.12.1) to the repeated successes the Roman general reported to Valens. See also MacDowall, *Adrianople, 378*, pp. 57–59.

92 Among the many possible evaluations of the size and composition of Valens's army, I have found it prudent to follow MacDowall's minimalist estimate in his *Adrianople, 378*, perhaps revising it upward a bit in view of Hoffmann's considerations below (see notes to chapter 9). Ammianus's assessment is in AM, 31.12.1.

IX. ADRIANOPLE, AUGUST 9, 378

The many available reconstructions of the battle of Adrianople are all based upon Ammianus Marcellinus's account and supplemented more or less conjecturally with analyses of the terrain and with the general information that has come down to us about the nature and organization of the late imperial army. In addition to the works cited in the introduction to the note section and in the notes to chapter 5, the specialist may wish to consult N. J. E. Austin, "Ammianus' Account of Adrianople: Some Strategic Observations," *L'Antiquité Classique* 15 (1972), pp. 301–9; T. H. S. Burns, "The Battle of Adrianople: A Reconsideration," *Historia* 22 (1973), pp. 336–45; and P. Richardot, *La Fin de l'armée romaine, 284–476* (Paris, 2001), pp. 271–91.

95 On Victor, see AM, 31.12.6, and Gregory of Nazianzus, *Letters*, 133–34; other information about Victor's career, which led him at one point to marry an Arab princess, can be found in Shahîd, *Byzantium and the Arabs in the Fourth Century*, pp. 164–69.

97 The invective against the barbarians who pretend to be Christians is in Eunapius, fragment 48.2.

101 On the *Notitia dignitatum*, see in general G. Clemente, *La Notitia Dignitatum* (Cagliari, 1968). Although available only in German and not easy to use, the weighty study by D. Hoffmann, *Das spätrömische Bewegungsheer und die Notitia Dignitatum*, 2 vols. (Düsseldorf, 1969–70), represents the most important attempt to analyze the *Notitia* for the purpose of extracting precise information about the personnel of the imperial army in the fourth century and also about, among other things, the units present at Adrianople. For the calculation according to which fourteen infantry units and two cavalry units were destroyed at Adrianople and not reconstituted, see pp. 449–57 of Hoffmann's book.

101 On the average size of the legions and the *auxilia*, see Hoffmann, *Das spätrömische Bewegungsheer,* p. 455; MacDowall, *Adrianople, AD 378*, pp. 22ff; and Richardot, *La Fin de l'armée romaine*, pp. 82–84.

107 For Bacurius, see the notes to chapter VI, second paragraph.

110 The citations come from AM, 31.13.2.

112 The casualty figures are those given in AM, 31.13.18.

112 The legend about Valens's death is reported not only by Ammianus (AM, 31.13.14–16) but also by the Christian historian Sozomen (6.40).

X. AFTER THE DISASTER

113 a huge emotional reaction throughout the Roman Empire: For two contemporary reactions, see Ammianus Marcellinus, 31.13.19 ("In the annals of our history, one can read of no battle, except for Cannae, that ended in such a massacre") and the Christian historian Rufinus, 1.13 ("this battle was the beginning of the ruin of the Roman Empire, then and later").

114 what they did to their prisoners, what they did to women: See, for example, AM, 31.6.7–8 and 8.7–8.

115 the ominous signs that had presaged Valens's death: AM, 31.1 and 31.15.8–9.

117 The story of the monk Isaac and his prediction is in Sozomen, 6.40. St. Ambrose's warning to Gratian is in Ambrose, *De fide ad Gratianum*, 2.16. Libanius's oration: 24.

120 that Goths should not make war on walls: "pacem sibi esse cum parietibus" (AM, 31.6.4).

120 "like wild animals made more ferocious by the exciting smell of blood": AM, 31.15.2.

122 a *candidatus* . . . sent on a mission to Syria: The story is in Jerome, *Vita Hilarionis*, 22.

123 "with their tribal medicine": AM, 31.16.1 ("artesque medendi gentiles").

125 The Saracen episode is in AM, 31.16.5–6.

XI. THEODOSIUS

129 On Theodosius's character, see S. Williams and G. Friell, *Theodosius: The Empire at Bay* (New Haven, 1998). On his approach to the Gothic problem, see M. Pavan, *La politica di Teodosio nella pubblicistica del suo tempo* (Roma, 1964).

130 For the Edict of Thessalonica issued in 380, see *Codex Theodosianus*, 16.1.2 (and see the final note to chapter I, above); for the edicts of 391–92, see *Codex Theodosianus*, 16.10.10–12.

130 Theodosius's edicts on army enlistments are in *Codex Theodosianus*, 7.13.8–11, 18.2–8, 22.9–11.

131 The chief sources for Athanaric's relations with Theodosius are the rhetorician Themistius, 15, and the later (sixth century) Byzantine historian Zosimus, 4.34.

132 Theodosius's peace accords with the various Gothic chieftains are analyzed in all the principal works dedicated to the conflict between the empire and the Goths and cited in the introduction to these notes; see also E. Demougeot, "Modalités d'établissement des fédérés barbares de Gratien et de Théodose," in *Mélanges W. Seston* (Paris, 1974), pp. 143–60; the same author's *La formation de l'Europe et les invasions barbares*, vol. 2, *De l'avènement de Dioclétien (284) à l'occupation germanique de l'Empire romain d'Occident (début du VIe siècle)* (Paris, 1979); and F. Ausbüttel, "Die Dedition der Westgoten vom 382 und ihre historische Bedeutung," *Athenaeum* 66 (1988), pp. 604–13.

Readers interested in further investigating the scarce, contradictory sources that shed some light, however dim, on this rather obscure topic can start with Eunapius, fragment 45.3, move to the later Zosimus, book 4, and then to the even later Jordanes, the Gothic historian of the sixth century (*Getica*, 27). Likewise useful, if not more so, are the orations and panegyrics of contemporary rhetoricians, in particular Themistius, 16 and 34; Libanio, 19; *Panegyrici Latini*, 2.

Themistius's discourse 16 is the one in which he heaps praise on Saturninus; on this extensively studied subject, and more generally on the humanitarian rhetoric typical of this period and of this milieu, see Pavan, *La politica di Teodosio nella pubblicistica del suo tempo*; G. Dagron, "L'Empire Romain d'Orient et les traditions politiques de l'Hellenisme: Le témoignage de Thémistios," *Travaux et mémoires* 3 (1968), pp. 104–16; X. L. W. Daly, "The Mandarin and the Barbarian: The Response of Themistius to the Gothic Challenge," *Historia* 21 (1972), pp. 351–79; and F. Heim, "Clémence ou extermination: Le pouvoir impérial et les barbares au IVe siècle," *Ktema* 17 (1992), pp. 281–95.

134 The excerpt from Pacatus is in *Panegyrici Latini*, 2.32–33.

134 The tale of the barbarian . . . was told again and again: See, for example, Claudian: "the errant Sarmatian comes to swear allegiance to you, the Goth casts off his animal skins and joins up, the Alan yields to Latin customs" (*4 Cons. Hon.*, 485–87), while the Germans of the Rhine have "enlisted in the military as our allies, and the Sicambri, having cut off their flowing locks, serve beneath our banners" (*In Eutr.*, 1.381–83).

135 For the stones of Concordia, see G. Lettich, *Le iscrizioni sepolcrali tardoantiche di Concordia* (Trieste, 1983).

135 They all have Flavius as a first name: Actually, the name Flavius tended to be attached to all those who exercised any sort of military or administrative function in the empire, including the lowest ranks of the army, so that the bearer of the name, which replaced his own, could well be a native of the empire—a worker in a local administration, for example. When, however, the name Flavius is accompanied by a second, recognizably barbarian name, it's obvious that the person in question was an immigrant integrated into imperial society. See the recent work of B. Salway, "What's in a Name? A Survey of Roman Onomastic Practice from c. 700 BC to AD 700," *Journal of Roman Studies* 84 (1994), pp. 137–40.

XII. THE ANTIBARBARIAN REACTION

137 For the clashes between regular army units and barbarian contingents in Roman service, see Zosimus, 4.30 and 4.40; in addition to these, the no less frequent conflicts between Gothic mercenaries and the civilian population should be considered, for example, in Libanius, 19.22, 20.14; in Sozomen, 7.25; and in Claudian, *In Eutr.*, 2.

138 The passage from Jerome is in his commentary on the Book of Daniel, 2.40. The dialogue between Ambrose and Magnus Maximus is in Ambrose, *Letters*, 24.4.

139 **In Syriac . . . the word for "soldier" became *Goth*:** Carrié, "L'esercito," p. 479 (see notes to chap. V, third paragraph).

139 Synesius expounds his views on the Huns in various works, particularly in *Catastasis* (*Patrologia Graeca* 66, col. 1576) and in *Letters*, 78; his invectives against the ineffectiveness of the regular army and the incompetence of its generals abound in *Letters*,

78, 95, 104, 107, 110, 122, 125, 130, and 132, and in *Catastasis* (*Patrologia Graeca* 66, col. 1567).

140 The long passage in which Synesius warns against the Goths who have entered the empire through the fault of Theodosius occurs in his treatise addressed to the emperor's son Arcadius: *De Regno*, 14–15. This text has been widely discussed and commented on; see, in particular, P. J. Heather, "The Anti-Scythian Tirade of Synesius' *De Regno*," *Phoenix* 42 (1988), pp. 152–72, and A. Cameron and J. Long, *Barbarians and Politics at the Court of Arcadius* (Berkeley, 1993), pp. 102–42.

141 For some time, historians have been pointing out the limits and contradictions of the so-called antibarbarian reaction, which seems to have been an aspect of the struggle for power and of the clashes between interest groups at the imperial court rather than the fruit of a real ideological intransigence. In addition to the works cited just above, see Pavan, *La politica di Teodosio nella pubblicistica del suo tempo*; F. Paschoud, *Roma Aeterna. Études sur le patriotisme romain dans l'Occident latin à l'époque des grandes invasions* (Rome, 1967); W. N. Bayless, "Anti-Germanism in the Age of Stilicho," *Byzantine Studies* 32 (1976), pp. 70–76; G. Albert, *Goten in Konstantinopel* (Paderborn, 1984); and E. P. Gluschanin, "Die Politik Theodosius' I. und die Hintergründe des sogenannten Anti-germanismus im oströmischen Reich," *Historia* 38 (1989), pp. 224–49.

143 On Fravitta, see Zosimus, 5.20–21.

143 On Alaric, in addition to the general works on the Goths cited in the introduction to these notes, see S. Mazzarino, *Stilicone: La crisi imperiale dopo Teodosio* (Rome, 1942), pp. 183–94; A. Cameron, *Poetry and Propaganda at the Court of Honorius* (Oxford, 1970), pp.

157–76; J. W. Liebeschuetz, "Alaric's Goths: Nation or Army?" in *Fifth-Century Gaul: A Crisis of Identity?* ed. J. F. Drinkwater and H. W. Elton (Cambridge, 1992), pp. 75–83; S. Giorcelli Bersani, *Romani e Barbari. Incontro e scontro di culture* (Torino, 2004).

146 The subject of the transfer of barbarian *foederati* to the western empire after the sack of Rome has been much discussed in recent years, beginning with the publication of the controversial book by W. Goffart, *Barbarians and Romans, A.D. 418–584: The Techniques of Accommodation* (Princeton, 1980). The reader who wishes to reconstruct the debate can start with the recent contributions of J. W. Liebeschuetz, "Cities, Taxes and the Accommodation of the Barbarians: The Theories of Durliat and Goffart," in *Kingdoms of the Empire: The Integration of Barbarians in Late Antiquity*, ed. W. Pohl (Leiden / New York / Köln, 1997), pp. 135–52, and, in the same volume, E. Chrysos, "De foederatis iterum," pp. 185–206.

INDEX

Index

Index